# Cocktail Party Priest

## A True Story of Friendship, Betrayal and Triumph

## RAYN RANDOM

COCKTAIL PARTY PRIEST
Rayn Random

© 2011 Rayn Random

First Edition January 2012

ISBN 13 PRINT: 978-0-9849729-0-6
ISBN 13 E-BOOK: 978-0-9849729-1-3

Published by
The Random Company
P.O. Box 2445
Monterey, CA 93942

Printed in the United States of America

To order print or digital copies of this book:
www.TheRandomCompany.net

*For Walter and Clifford*
*Faithful partners for 47 years*

# CONTENTS

# CHAPTER ONE

# In the Beginning

*"And, I mean no disrespect by this, but were you born biologically female?"*

I had never before met the man who asked me that question, and my natural response would have been an immediate departure. Although I instantly seethed with indignation, I had to keep my emotions under control and unexposed. The patient, quizzical expression revealed by the questioner seated across from me was as innocent appearing as if he'd asked me where I'd had lunch the day before. For a moment, I reflexively closed my eyes as though he'd struck me, and in a way, he had. When I opened them, I looked directly at him and calmly answered, "Yes." The man was an attorney representing the priest of my Episcopal Church, and I was under oath in pre-trial discovery.

If I had been an accused woman in a 1692 Salem courtroom, the question might have been, "Were you born a heretic, or did you change yourself into one?" For years, the priest had accused me of tormenting him, causing him great fear, pain, and suffering without relief. I was condemned within the church, denied the sacraments, and everywhere I went in society, I was shunned and made a subject of derision and speculation. My protests were ignored, or met with condescending sneers of impatience. Three centuries later, little had changed except that I would not be burned at the stake.

In January, 1990, my husband of 27 years and my beloved step-father suffered massive strokes within five days of each other. My step-father lived for thirty days. My husband, Ralph, survived, but was totally paralyzed on his right side and unable to speak.

2 - Rayn Random

Making his situation even more tragic, his left hand and part of his arm had been blown off during a combat mission when he was 22 years old. Losing his "other" hand was a fear he'd lived with all of his adult life. A tall, healthy man until that day, he was now physically helpless, and he lived the last seven and a half years of his life in a VA hospital.

But, all was not gloom and tears during the years that he was ill. Until he could no longer sit in a wheelchair, I took him to lunch at the commissary and for walks around the hospital grounds with our German Shepherd dog, Max, walking beside Ralph's wheelchair. On the weekends when very few people were around and the commissary was closed, our walks were longer and we sometimes came upon wet sidewalk cement because the hospital was always expanding. Before we turned to go back, we would have some fun with it. I would draw a little heart in one corner with our initials inside of it. The following weekend, when the concrete had dried, we would return to our crime scene and paint the heart red with nail polish. When the color faded, we painted the hearts again. Over the years as we took our walks, Ralph always remembered where our hearts were and we would stop to fondly admire our handiwork. I'm sure most of them are still there, but no longer red.

We had developed our own way of communicating that was about 90 percent understood between us, but I did most of the talking, and as we walked, I often sang for him. Sometimes, we even "argued" like the still-married couple that we were. The only difference was that I always got the last word, which made Ralph laugh. We found many things to enjoy in our private world, and nothing changed the fact that we still loved each other as much as ever, maybe even more. Ralph died 27 days before our 35th wedding anniversary.

At the time of Ralph's stroke, I had returned to college and was studying law to become a paralegal. Only six months were left of the two years, so I stayed in school and got a part time job to pay the rent on Ralph's office, anticipating that I would use it when I set up my paralegal business. I managed to finish school with my 4.0 still intact and received an award for outstanding achievement. I was even invited to study at Oxford, and I would have loved to go, but I needed to concentrate on my husband's care, my mother's diminishing health, and establishing my new business.

In spite of my mixed feelings, I was glad that I'd kept Ralph's office. I left his paintings on the walls, kept his desk, and the gooseneck lamp that really did look like a goose, but bought a few new pieces of furniture. There was just one more thing that had to be done—the most difficult of all—I had to take Ralph's nameplate off the door and replace it with mine. I gathered my emotions and waited until everyone else had left their offices for the day, so they wouldn't see me crying.

By then, my mother required 24 hour care, so the following years were devoted to Ralph, to work, and to her. I eventually got re-acquainted with old friends and made new ones, but nothing was the same as it had been before, and I knew in my heart that it never would be. The ten years following Ralph's stroke had drastically changed my life and my home—Palo Alto.

My family had settled there a hundred years earlier when my grandfather was teaching physics at Stanford, and my father had been born in Palo Alto. Even though I grew up elsewhere, when my mother remarried and I arrived in Palo Alto for the first time, I knew that I had finally come "home."

Ralph and I lived in what's called "Old Palo Alto"—the street in front of our house still had a horse drawn carriage turnaround in the middle of the street that made a perfect playground for the neighborhood children. We were a close community and the city as a whole preferred to avoid attention and to remain as it had always been. It offered the best of both worlds, a wonderful place to live and raise a family, but close to big city entertainment and shopping in San Francisco.

When Ralph and I were dating, we went to San Francisco almost every weekend for hotel dining, or to enjoy the counter at Vesuvio's where we could watch the cooks and drink the house wine. There were theatres offering plays and musicals, wonderful restaurants, and live entertainment at the clubs in North Beach such as The Purple Onion and the Hungry I, where many famous entertainers got their starts. We could walk around Union Square and stroll along Market Street without being harassed.

San Francisco was no longer the wonderful place it had been, and Palo Alto had changed drastically while I wasn't looking. Business founders and executives who became overnight millionaires in the sky-rocketing Silicon Valley technology boom wanted to live in Palo Alto. Because there was no land for expansion, the land, rather than the house built on it, became the valuable commodity. Historic houses in my neighborhood, standing when I'd left for my office in the morning, were frequently gone when I returned home, leaving not a scrap of shattered wood to remind neighbors of what had existed there only hours earlier. They disappeared with such frequency that I often couldn't remember which particular house had been there in the morning. What came to be called monster houses with multi-million dollar price tags replaced them, and traffic became a frustration every hour of the day. It seemed as though half the people living on the San Francisco Peninsula came to Palo Alto to shop, have lunch, and enjoy the evening and weekend entertainment. Every place was so crowded that if I didn't get errands completed by 11:00 a.m., there would be nowhere to park.

I was burning out, getting restless, and felt that I no longer belonged in Palo Alto. When I walked Max at night and saw closely what had happened to my neighborhood, the restless feeling grew into a certainty that Palo Alto was no longer the place for me. It had nothing more to hold me.

While chatting on the phone with a friend, I heard myself say that I was moving to Monterey. I was as surprised as she was, and I don't know to this day why I chose Monterey, except that I had been there—the only time—on a stormy December weekend two years earlier to complete five dives for scuba certification. The ocean had been in her wild, winter glory that entire weekend and forced cancellation of our last two dives, but the excitement of the huge waves and roiling water reminded me of summers I'd spent at my grandparents' home on Lake Winnebago in Wisconsin. I'd always loved the waves and whitecaps that the frequent storms created, and maybe the water is what drew me to Monterey.

Whatever the reason, I immediately began to turn that spontaneous decision into a reality, and I drove the 80 miles to Monterey to find my new home. I bought the first house I looked at, and within a month I had closed my paralegal office and put my house on the market. There was no turning back.

# CHAPTER TWO

# Exodus

Before Ralph and I were married and during the first year of our marriage, we'd attended a small, old, traditional Episcopal Church. It looked as though it had been transported directly from a flowering English countryside, and the old priest right along with it. After our son was born, we had him baptized in that church—named for my step-father who'd had no children— and he became an Episcopalian just like his grandfather. Sadly, within less than two years, every trace of that lovely church was gone. Progress tore it down and replaced it with a hideous, grey, concrete monstrosity having no resemblance to a church on the outside—or the inside. The very spirit of the church seemed to have deserted it, and we became infrequent churchgoers. But, after I'd settled in Monterey, I wanted to return to an Episcopal church like that one, if such a church still existed.

As a child I had been baptized and confirmed in the Lutheran Church, but in college I often went with a friend to an Episcopal Church and found that I preferred it. I liked the more formal service, the 1928 *Book of Common Prayer*, and I treasured the traditions such as kneeling to pray and standing to sing. It seemed more appropriate in a gathering devoted to God, and from then forward, I considered myself to be an Episcopalian.

Because I'm not a morning person, my new church had to have a late service. Looking in the Monterey phone book, I discovered one that was less than ten minutes from my house and happily, it had a 10:30 AM service. When I went the following Sunday, I remembered most of the ritual from the years before and, although I had to keep flipping pages in my prayer book to keep up, the experience left me feeling wonderful.

The more than 100 year old church was a small, typical, English, country church which also bore architectural reminders that it was built in historic Spanish California. The priest, Fr. Alan Wolter, was an older gentleman who had come out of retirement to keep the church going while a committee searched for a new rector. And, like the priest at the church in Palo Alto, he was kindly, charming, and the perfect priest for that church, although I held my breath whenever he had to get up from his knees at the altar. Attendance was slim, and much of the congregation seemed to be aging along with their priest.

I had never been one to join the other members for coffee, or to become involved in church activities outside of the Sunday morning service. My practice had always been to get there just before the doors closed, sit in the back, not to chat with neighbors other than a brief hello, give as generously as possible, ignore the invitation to sign the guest book on the way out, thank the priest, and leave quickly while politely declining invitations to come to coffee hour. Return the following Sunday. Repeat.

That worked just fine until Fr. Wolter asked for people to help with the Blessing of the Animals. As an animal lover, and having always had multiple pets, I couldn't resist volunteering. Never having attended a church that performed the animal blessing, I imagined it would be a lot of fun, which it was. On the day of the blessing, everyone sat in the sunny courtyard, and the pet personalities were as varied as the people who'd brought them. Each pet got a little medal and a treat. Naturally, being a church, we took up a collection—for the local animal shelter. I'd left my young German Shepherds, Bravo and Carlota, in the car because I was afraid they would want to personally and enthusiastically greet everyone, frightening some of the shyer pets. Fr. Wolter and Fr. Politzer, a retired rector who'd come back to help, refused to leave them out and blessed them through the open car windows.

What had been a very enjoyable and unique afternoon for

me had an unanticipated consequence. I had became friendly with some of the other parishioners, and that set a precedent that opened the door to participating in more than the Sunday service, although that didn't happen until the fall of the following year.

Each Sunday, one of the priest candidates being considered for employment by St. John's came to conduct the service and deliver that day's sermon. Having nothing to do with the procedure and wanting no involvement of any kind, I had no opinion about them and paid no particular attention to any of them. I followed my usual habit—say hello, sing, pray, give an offering, say something nice to the priest on the way out, and leave immediately.

In January of 2001, six months after I'd joined St. John's, Fr. William Martin arrived from the Bahamas to be our new rector. As one might expect, he had some adjustment difficulties at the beginning, but with the help of several long-term members who had selected him and wanted him to succeed, he became well-liked and popular with the congregation. It pleased me that the congregation was so happy to have him, and I believed that his arrival would bring a new life to the church, but I kept to my usual Sunday procedure. I thought that our new priest's somewhat intellectual sermons were outstanding and they always held my attention, but I had no desire to hang around and chat with him after services as so many others were eager to do. I had more important chats to attend to, and that was meeting friends for our regular Sunday brunch.

In time, word got around that St. John's had a new priest and a breath of new life that attracted old members to return and brought new ones. The congregation felt more connected, but I still avoided any involvement other than Sunday services. In August, eight months after Fr. Martin's arrival, the church women held their annual fund raiser, a typical church rummage sale. One of the women I'd met at the blessing of the animals asked me to help and because she was such a nice person—always so warm and friendly toward me—I couldn't refuse.

During the preparations and on the day of the sale, I had the opportunity to observe Fr. Martin with the other members of the congregation. He was enthusiastic and appreciative of everything we were doing, and it turned out to be a very successful day for St. John's. Just before closing time, he asked two other women and me to set up a table with snacks in the conference room. He wanted to celebrate, and when the customers departed and the doors to the sale were shut, several bottles of wine appeared and we had a party. No one expressed the slightest concern that it might be inappropriate to enjoy wine outside of the Communion offering, and from then on wine was served at church dinners. People who had never chatted with each other before engaged in lively conversations like old friends and had second—maybe even third—servings of wine. A good time was had by all.

Fr. Martin was clearly not the usual staid, priestly persona that everyone had known in the past. He was then almost forty, about the same age as my son, good-looking, intelligent, and he had a very relaxed and entertaining charm. He was not married, although the Episcopal Church allows its priests to marry and even encourages it. His enthusiasm for the church and the congregation made everyone feel as though they were an important part of the church body, and that gave us a lot to celebrate at St. John's Chapel.

In October, Fr. Martin invited me to dinner at the rectory,[1] a condominium the church had purchased for him in Carmel. He was known to be an accomplished chef, and the dinner was excellent. He also invited Bravo and Carlota, I suppose as sort of canine chaperones since he had no other guests. I brought their big towels to put on the floor indicating where they were supposed to lie down, and they behaved like angels, appropriate when one is the guest of a priest.

After dinner, Fr. Martin and I sat in the living room and

---

1      A priest's home is referred to as the "rectory," and is often owned by the church.

discussed St. John's and his plans for its future. I volunteered to help all that I could, including offering the use of my house for occasional church get-togethers. St. John's was everything that I believed a church should be and its revival was very important to me, almost a mission. During our conversation, while we were still talking about St Johns, Fr. Martin said something that took me by surprise.

He said that he personally knew homosexual priests in the Episcopal Church who had married straight women to conceal the fact that they were gay. He stated that he believed it was a terrible thing to do and the consequences were devastating when the truth was revealed. He said that he would never do such a thing and had chosen to be celibate. He continued on that subject and revealed a great deal about himself and his past that was very personal—almost confessional. Although it surprised me to be taken into his confidence so suddenly, what he told me made no difference to me then, nor does it now. The evening ended early, and it was the beginning of an enjoyable and pleasant friendship. I seldom thought of that conversation and never related it to anyone else.

By the end of the year, at Fr. Martin's instigation, I had become a member of the Altar Guild and on his nomination, I'd been elected to the Vestry, the governing body of the church that's comparable to a board of directors. St. John's had become an important part of my life, but I had other interests as well. I was a Court Appointed Special Advocate for abused, neglected, and abandoned children, served on the Monterey Opera board and an Arts Council Committee, and had joined a women's organization. I belonged to a club where I worked out regularly and had wonderful friends. My life was interesting, satisfying, and fun.

In December I had a Christmas party at my home and invited several parishioners, along with personal friends that I had made outside of church. Fr. Martin offered to cook, so I accepted the proposal and left the menu up to him. A few days before the party, he and a young Naval Postgraduate School (NPS) student from Texas named Scott, who often served as an acolyte, put up my Christmas tree and decorated it for me. Fr. Martin barbequed dinner out on the deck, and we had a delightful evening. He asked me, as well as Scott and other friends, to call him Bill when we were not around other church members.

Fr. Martin had no ornaments for his Christmas tree at the rectory, so I loaned him the ones belonging to my parents. I was glad they would be on someone's tree, but I didn't want it to be mine. The previous ten years had been difficult, and by then my mother was also deceased. I wanted to live in the future, not the past, and seeing the ornaments a time or two at the rectory with other people celebrating Christmas would be perfect.

Fr. Martin's brother visited him for the holidays, and the three of us spent an evening at my house having dinner, listening to the *Messiah*, exchanging gifts, and taking photos by the Christmas tree. I gave Fr. Martin a signed, Waterford crystal cross. He gave me a book that he inscribed, and "J'adore" perfume. No platonic male friend had ever given me perfume—a rather personal gift—but I didn't want to embarrass him by refusing it, and that idea seemed a little outdated. On Christmas day, Fr. Martin had a church party at the rectory. All of my parents' ornaments were on his tree, and I enjoyed them without dwelling on memories of the past.

It was a wonderful Christmas for everyone, and I looked forward to 2002.

CHAPTER THREE

# Where Two or Three Are Gathered Together

In 2002, St John's attendance grew at both of the Sunday morning services, and I was thrilled with its rebirth for which I credited Fr. Martin. Among the new members were Jo and Dale Howard who began participating almost as soon as they arrived from a nearby Episcopal church. Jo was very active in the community and had a wide circle of friends. Dale was a well-respected attorney. I got to know Jo when she joined the Altar Guild and I liked her a lot. She read bible passages as part of the Sunday services, and she and Dale served together as ushers, which was a delight to watch. Jo was a great-looking, high energy person, and Dale was handsome and reserved. They were enthusiastically welcomed at St. John's.

Scott Jackson's fiancé came from Texas to visit him regularly, and they were often dinner guests at my house along with Fr. Martin. We became close enough friends that they invited me to their Texas wedding. Jo and Dale were also invited, and Fr. Martin had been invited to assist in the ceremony. The wedding and festivities would be a smashing affair and I looked forward to going.

When there were church gatherings at my house or the rectory, Fr. Martin and I helped each other with them. I had a few dinner parties for 30 people and a large Thanksgiving dinner, for which Fr. Martin did most of the cooking each time, sharing the cost. As a result of the entertaining, I became quite good friends with several church members. We attended many of the same community events, and had numerous non-church friends in common.

Everything in my life was going very well until February, when a neighbor claimed that my dogs had attacked her. They had not attacked her, but she filed a lawsuit against me—her husband is an attorney. My insurance company told me that because of a terrible case in San Francisco in which a huge dog attacked and killed a woman, they were getting a lot of copy-cat claims regarding large dogs, and they hired an attorney to represent me

The woman's husband and his associate attorney notified me that they were coming to my house to measure Bravo and Carlota. I was confident that my dogs would be their usual eagerly friendly selves, but nevertheless, I was concerned that the attorneys might deliberately provoke them during their "measuring" to support a claim that my dogs were vicious. I was in fact, terrified at the prospect and my dogs' reactions to being physically handled by two men who were strangers to them, not the friendly kind of strangers.

The measuring was on a Wednesday morning when I knew that Fr. Martin would be on his way to church, so I asked him to please stop by while the attorneys were present and he agreed without hesitation. I thought that having a priest witness the attorneys' conduct would keep them from any unfriendly actions with my dogs, or later false testimony. My attorney could not testify as a witness, so I needed a third party, and who better than a priest?

Around nine in the evening on the night before the measuring, I discovered a fax from Fr. Martin. He had never before sent me a fax. It read, "I am a priest and pastor. I am accountable to God and the church. I am called upon to run a church and to minister first and foremost to a congregation. I am sorry that I will not be able to be with you on Wednesday." The letter was on church stationery and signed, "Fr. William Martin." He'd always signed cards or notes "Bill."

I couldn't understand the tone of the letter, the official letterhead, the formal signature, or why he hadn't simply phoned me while there was still time to get someone else. He sometimes called me five times a day when he had problems. I'd stood by him, defended him when others chose not to, and helped him deal with things that worried him. His behavior was inexplicable, and it upset me that I'd been his friend and confidant when he needed one, but he wouldn't give me even fifteen minutes of his time when I needed help from him. He knew my dogs very well and he knew how much they meant to me. I couldn't understand his sudden, distant attitude. I knew of nothing that would have prompted it, and it left me bewildered and very worried about the next morning.

The measuring took place without incident, and a medical report that we later subpoenaed showed that the woman had not been bitten. In fact, the treatment recommended by her doctor had been to go home and take two Advil. That was a huge relief, but it didn't excuse Fr. Martin's refusing to help me, and I was still perplexed by his letter. I was angry, too, because I had devoted so much time, effort, and money to the church and yet, the church's pastor wouldn't do the small favor that he had to know was so important to me.

In fact, to my amazement, he stopped speaking to me altogether. Someone told me it was because we were "too close," whatever that meant. I didn't think there was any difference in our friendship from the others that he had, or that I'd previously had with platonic male friends. I had not instigated the friendship, and if it had become "too close," I was not aware of it, I had not pursued it, and I thought that society had progressed enough that men and women could be friends without any suggestion of romantic involvement. Because of my old habit of always departing immediately after Sunday services, I had never been aware of the jealousy, envy, and downright viciousness that exist in churches.

There were other Episcopal churches nearby, and staying at St. John's wasn't worth the problem it was apparently causing.

I decided to simply go to a different Episcopal Church. So, I resigned from my positions by letter without giving any reason. I felt no obligation to explain myself and if I had, what would I have said? After attending several other churches on different Sundays, I realized that St. John's was the only one that used the 1928 *Book of Common Prayer* that I knew and loved so much. In fact, the others seldom used even the newer 1978 version. At some of them, the whole service was printed out like a restaurant menu, and I was horrified at how casual they were. I wondered where God was on those Sunday mornings because he seemed to have been almost forgotten.

Leaving St. John's had been a big mistake, and to make matters worse, no one knew the reason why I had left. It finally occurred to me that my sudden departure had probably fueled even more speculation. Someone at St. John's needed to know the reason, so I called my friend Gaby who was also on the Altar Guild, and asked her to meet me at Clint Eastwood's Mission Ranch restaurant in Carmel. We sat outdoors on the veranda, watching the sheep in the pasture and the ocean in the distance, as I explained my reason for leaving. She told me that people missed me, and she urged me to come back. I admitted regretting my hasty departure, and it didn't take much persuading before I agreed to return.

My position on the Altar Guild was still open, but Fr. Martin had already appointed Gaby to replace me on the Vestry. Not long after my return, as Gaby and I were working in the church kitchen, she said that she had told Fr. Martin—in advance—that I intended to come back. He'd replied that I could come back, but "there can't be any more of that romantic stuff." I was outraged at the very thought that I needed his permission to return to my own church, but I was stunned at his comment about "romantic stuff." I was, in fact, almost speechless. There it was again—the notion that there was some sort of romance going on—only now, it wasn't just "too close," he had escalated it to "romantic stuff." I couldn't imagine what made him say such a bizarre thing and why he would choose to say it to Gaby.

Gaby is a very gentle person, so I didn't argue with her for something Fr. Martin had said. I told her that there had been no romantic stuff and let it go. It stuck in my mind though, and I still couldn't comprehend why he knowingly and deliberately gave her such a wrong impression. It turned out that "wrong impression" was an enormous understatement because of the far worse things he was saying about me behind my back that were spreading like the spores of a sickening mold—not only at St. John's—but all over the Monterey Peninsula. He had begun his malicious campaign against me within months of our acquaintance, and no one ever told me the hate-filled lies he'd spread about me until more than two years later.

In the spring of 2002, Scott Jackson completed his studies at the NPS and would soon be leaving to get married before his transfer to another post. On his last Sunday at St. John's, his fiancé joined him and they stayed for coffee hour after the service. I had a question about my computer that I knew Scott could answer, so we briefly stepped aside to discuss it. He was polite to me—as Navy officers are trained to be—but not at all like the Scott I'd entertained in my home so many times before. His fiancé avoided even looking in my direction and did not speak to me, nor acknowledge my presence. When everyone said good-bye and wished them well, she, again, neither spoke to me, nor looked at me. I couldn't help but wonder if I had done something to offend her, but she had been in Texas since our last meeting and had been her usual friendly self while enjoying my hospitality. When I did not receive a formal invitation to the wedding, I knew for certain that I was no longer invited, but I didn't have the slightest idea why. I knew the wedding had not been postponed, as Fr. Martin happily announced to the congregation that he would be participating at the Jackson wedding and we would have a substitute priest the following Sunday.

Five years later, Jo Howard testified, "He (Fr. Martin) said, 'Scott, you cannot invite Rayn Random. She cannot be at the wedding because she is a problem. She's stalking me, and I cannot possibly be there and be a part of it if Rayn Random is there.'" What prompted Fr. Martin to commence his vicious campaign against me is still an unanswered mystery to me. The only prior things that I was aware had occurred were his failure to show up for the dog measuring and my leaving St. John's.

After I'd returned, we still didn't speak, and I'd avoided any encounters with him until one Sunday in August at coffee hour when he suddenly hurried over to me and breathlessly said, "Rayn! It's Martha's birthday next week and we have to do something for her." We hadn't spoken to each other in six months, but he acted as though nothing had ever been wrong and for a moment, I didn't know how to respond. While I hesitated, it crossed my mind that it would be nice to have civility again because avoiding him was more difficult than being polite. I especially liked Martha, and we'd sometimes had dinner with her. It would be nice to celebrate for her, so I agreed.

On the day of her birthday, while Fr. Martin and I were in my kitchen preparing our celebration dinner before she arrived, he apologized—twice—for his behavior. I was still completely unaware of what he was saying about me behind my back and that he was the reason I had been uninvited to the wedding. Knowing nothing else, I assumed he was referring to the dog measuring, and I accepted the apologies. After that, I jokingly referred to it as our "incommunicado" period, and everything went well from then on.

In early November, 2002, my friend Adrianne introduced me to Carole Dooley, who would become one of my very closest friends. Adrianne, a stunningly beautiful woman, tall, with black hair, clear blue eyes, creamy light skin, and always glamorously dressed, is very active within almost every charitable organization on the Monterey Peninsula. She can be seen at most social events.

On this occasion, an Authors' Table dinner fundraiser, she was a volunteer chef and needed the assistance of two servers, so she asked Carole and me to help her, affectionately referring to us as her "two blondes." Authors' Table dinners are held at various private homes around the Peninsula, and each one features a well known author as the guest speaker. Wine, cocktails, and conversation precede a lavish meal for as many guests as the host or hostess can comfortably seat at beautifully appointed tables. The guests purchase tickets ranging from $150 to $500 per person, and the funds raised support reading and writing programs for students.

Fr. Martin arrived wearing his clerical collar, and it was my assumption that the hostess or Adrianne had invited him as her guest. The dinner was superb, beautifully presented, and the guests were very congenial and animated, talking easily with each other before and during dinner. The author of the evening was Dr. Laina Farhat Holzman, a firsthand authority on the Middle East, particularly Iran and Islam. I'd heard her speak many times before, and she always gave well researched and thoughtful lectures. This evening, she spoke while standing at her place at the head of the long table that seated sixteen. After she had discussed her recent book and guests were asking questions, Fr. Martin, seated near the other end of the table, began to make outrageous anti-Semitic statements that were overheard by everyone, and the shock of his statements quickly silenced all conversation down the entire table.

I wasn't paying particular attention while Carole and I collected the desert plates until suddenly, a Jewish couple seated next to Laina stood up and the wife declared to everyone that they had never been so insulted. They immediately left, while the poor, horrified hostess followed them with profuse apologies. The host of the evening was also Jewish, and it was a dreadful embarrassment for everyone except Fr. Martin, who seemed puzzled by all the concern over what he'd said. He simply asked for another Scotch—"Black Label."

Carole attended St. John's with Adrianne a few times after the Authors' Table, and I chatted with her at coffee afterward. We were both widows and discovered that we had many more things in common other than the trauma of a husband's death. We soon became close friends.

At Christmas, as we had done the year before, Fr. Martin and his brother had dinner at my house and we exchanged gifts. The rest of the holiday was celebrated at church or for parishioners at the rectory, where my parents' ornaments were again on Fr. Martin's tree. On Christmas Eve the church was filled to capacity, and there were now enough children in the Sunday school to put on a Christmas pageant. While Fr. Martin's brother and I waited for the service to begin, people were still arriving, and folding chairs were being set up in the back for the overflow. It was answered prayers, and I remember looking around and wondering what walls could be moved to make room for our growing congregation. St. John's had come back to life exactly as I'd hoped it would, and it looked as though a wonderful new year was approaching. Had someone predicted what devastation the next four years would bring to me, I would have thought that person an incredible fool.

On February 28, 2003, the week of Fr. Martin's birthday, and at his request, we had a dinner party at my house, although he insisted that his birthday would not be mentioned. Half of the guests would be his and half would be mine, along with a few mutual friends from church. Three of Fr. Martin's guests were Ukrainian military officers who were studying at the Naval Postgraduate School's Defense Resources Management Institute. One of the men had previously given me his business card at Fr. Martin's house and invited me to visit his family if I ever journeyed to the Ukraine. The card, written in Russian on one side and English on the other, stated that he was an assistant professor at the Institute of Strategic Studies at the Military Academy in Brno. Although Fr. Martin referred to them as his students, he was actually their local social host whose job was to entertain and show them around during their three month stay in Monterey. They resided at the Naval School.

Fr. Martin had to take a doctorate program exam the day of the party, which left everything to me. So, I decided to make it a sit-down dinner for eighteen people, the most that I could accommodate that way. It was a perfect chance to do what I especially enjoy, and that's cooking and entertaining friends. I make a pretty good pot roast, so that's what I chose to serve, with browned potatoes, browned onion halves, carrots, and silky beef gravy, a true American dinner.

In the early afternoon of the party, Carole came by to drop off a portable oven that I had asked to borrow. She offered to help me, but stayed only briefly because there was nothing to do as everything was right on schedule or already done. She then left on some errands, stopping at the little market down the hill from my house, where she encountered Fr. Martin who was waiting in the checkout line, holding two packages wrapped in white paper from the meat department. When she asked him what he was up to, he said that he was buying ham hocks for pea soup and held up each of his packages.

He cautioned her, "Don't you tell a soul. Every time it's this woman's turn to make soup for my Sunday soup sale, I have to remake it because her recipe is so terrible." Then he sighed, "What a day! Before I can get to the soup, I have to go all the way up to Rayn's house to help her with her party. She was on the phone to me, crying and all upset because she just can't handle it alone. I had to promise her I'd go up and help her so she would stop crying."

Carole said that she turned to look directly at him and asked, "Really?"

He greeted her question with his eyes directed upward as though it were too hard to explain and said, "You don't know the half of it."

Carole paused a moment to ascertain if he was joking or

serious. He was serious, and her response to him was, "I know that I just left Rayn's home less than a half hour ago, and everything is absolutely beautiful. Her tables are decorated and set with her beautiful China and crystal. She was browning the last of six pot roasts, and everything was under control." Then she looked straight at Martin and slowly said, "Father Martin, I asked if I could help, and Rayn said, 'No, everything is done.' She told me she was ready to sit down and have a cup of coffee. Everything for the party is beautiful, including the flowers she arranged last night." His face paled, and his eyes widened at the realization that Carole had called him in an obvious lie.

Dinner turned out perfectly and the compliments were wonderful. Everyone seemed to have an exceptionally good time, including me. Carole's date presented me with a dozen gardenias, Monica's husband John, a professional singer, serenaded me. Carole proposed a toast, and two of the Ukrainian students—the third one had to hurry to the hospital as his wife was about to deliver their second child—stood to thank me and toasted the evening. As he had requested, Fr. Martin's birthday, just three days earlier, was not mentioned. After all of the guests had departed, John went to bed and Monica and I washed glasses and flatware until one o'clock in the morning.

Fr. Martin and I never chatted at Sunday coffee so it wasn't until mid-week Communion that we spoke. Everything was as friendly as usual and after the service he said he'd come over to help me move a large glass outdoor table we'd used for the party. John had already moved it before he and Monica had left the next morning, so it wasn't necessary.

There was no phone call from Fr. Martin during the next few days as there normally would have been. I never called him except when it was necessary, or to return his calls, but I had a question that required an answer, so I phoned him. I left a message, and it surprised me that he didn't phone back as soon as he got it. He never did call, and it became apparent that we were back in "incommunicado" mode. I thought it was kind of silly behavior and casually wondered what had brought it on. Having no explanation from him, the only reason I could think of was that he probably had his nose out of joint because I'd gotten so much of the attention at the party. Usually he was the center of attention. Or, maybe he was disappointed that we didn't acknowledge his birthday, in spite of his instructions to me not to mention it. I gave it no more thought as I assumed that he'd get over whatever it was the same as he had before.

Fr. Martin had asked Carole to use her medical connections to help one of the students' wives—the one who'd had the baby— secure a medical position as she had been a physician in the Ukraine. Carole called in a favor and arranged an appointment for Svetlana at Salinas Valley Memorial Hospital. The next Sunday after church, I was with Carole as she told Vitali, the husband, about the appointment while Fr. Martin observed them from a distance. She gave Vitali her card with the information written on the back of it, and Fr. Martin immediately called him away. Vitali thanked Carole, and without putting her card in his pocket, he hurried to join Fr. Martin. They spoke briefly, and then Fr. Martin suddenly snatched Carole's card from Vitali's hand. The two of them immediately went into the church office, and Carole and I looked at each other in disbelief. Svetlana never did keep the appointment that Carole had made for her.

In mid-March I sent the February party photos to the people I knew, but I didn't know where to send those of the visiting students, or even the names of two of them. I was sure they would appreciate having the pictures of themselves to take home. I still hadn't heard from Fr. Martin and didn't want to phone him, so I decided to mail them to him at the rectory. Then, remembering his "romantic stuff" comment to Gaby, I became concerned about what exaggeration he might make of my even *mailing* the photos. Wanting to make it clear to him that there was no hidden intent in sending them, and to keep his imagination from taking off on another fantasy, I included the following note:

"Please give the February 28 dinner party photos to the appropriate people. It would be nice if you let them know that they are from me, not you, and that I truly enjoyed having them as guests in my home.

"The others are Christmas photos that you forgot to take with you previously.

"Please also restrain yourself from leaping to further fanciful conclusions because I have sent these photos. How unfortunate it is that you cannot understand that friendship, including gestures and expressions of affection by heterosexual men and women, are neither invitations, nor preludes, to more. You have nothing to fear except your own imagination."

Retaliation came swiftly.

# CHAPTER FOUR

# And the Lord Taketh Away

Not only did retaliation come swiftly, but the blows were forcefully delivered without warning or explanation. Each one taken separately was relatively unimportant, but together they constituted a deliberate pattern, and each was clearly intended to humiliate me publicly and send a message—leave St. John's. The first strike came the very next Sunday morning when Fr. Martin, while standing at the front row of pews, gave the weekly announcements to the congregation. He smiled at everyone and said that it gave him, "great pleasure," to announce that Gladys Shultz was our new flower chair. Until that stunning—at least for me—moment, I had been the flower chair. I had no idea that I was removed, or was about to be removed, until I heard it in the presence of the entire congregation. Fr. Martin, who had personally assigned me to the position, which was affirmed by a vote of the entire group of women, gave me no warning ahead of time because his clear intent was to embarrass and humiliate me as much as possible. When I wrote a letter asking him why he had dismissed me, I received no answer. As a twist of the knife, he followed it up with a repeat notice of my replacement in the weekly bulletin and in two letters. One letter went to the ECW[2] stating the same thing which, of course, they already knew, and he had the second letter read aloud—in my presence at different meeting—to people who already knew.

I was also Treasurer of the Altar Guild by Fr. Martin's appointment. Treasurer of *anything* isn't something that appealed

---

2     Episcopal Church Women: all women in the congregation are automatically considered to be members

to me, as I'm not even attentive to my own records, but the woman who had the job couldn't continue, so I had agreed to take it. I'd been handed a large cardboard box containing the "treasury" which had been stashed on the floor in an office. Before I had even straightened out the box, made a deposit, or written a single check, I received the second retaliation blow—by letter. Fr. Martin wrote it on official church stationery, with copies to five other people. He wrote four sentences:

"Please return all checkbooks, records and materials pertaining to the office of Altar Guild Treasurer to Ronnie at St. John's. We are meeting to choose a new treasurer. In the meantime, Barbara will be the sole signer on the account. Thank you for your cooperation."

No reason was given, no phone call, nothing, just the letter out of the blue one week after the flower announcement. The tone of the letter, its urgency, the fact that no reason was stated, and his sending it to five other people suggested that I couldn't be trusted with Altar Guild funds. I had given thousands of dollars to the church and spent my own money on many items for the church, including a commercial stove. I had never once asked to be reimbursed, even for the flowers I regularly bought on behalf of the Altar Guild. It was highly unlikely that I would tap into Altar Guild funds. The letter was a deliberate insult, intended to embarrass me—again.

I protested in a letter, copied to the same five people Fr. Martin had included, that read in part: "Your actions have been deliberate, unjustifiable and designed to hurt, insult and humiliate me publicly. *Your behavior as a friend is despicable. As a priest, it is unconscionable.*" Those last words would be quoted in a courtroom four years later. Needless to say, I never received an answer or an explanation.

I could feel the pressure Fr. Martin was applying in the hope that I would voluntarily leave. After all, I'd walked away from St. John's once before, so maybe I'd do it again if he made me uncomfortable and embarrassed enough. Not this time. My heels were dug in, and I wouldn't take the bait he was shoving in my direction. He would have to try harder, and he did—in a very strange way.

Churches have their own calendars marking special days, events, and religious seasons such as Easter, Lent, Pentecost and others. For each season, the colors on the altar and the priest's vestments change. Fr. Martin always wore a chasuble,[3] although some priests don't wear them at all. It was the custom at St. John's that a member of the Altar Guild stood at the rear of the church when the last hymn was sung and the choir returned, followed by the priest. The priest gave her—it was always a "her"—any books and papers he carried, and after removing his chasuble, he handed it to her.

It's always crowded at the back when the choir is assembled there, and the priest stands next to the recipient so he can simply hand over the chasuble. This time, Fr. Martin stood as far away from me as he could get, and after he took off the chasuble, he stood frozen in place with a terrified look on his face, staring at me wide-eyed as though he were afraid to get near me. I was looking at him, waiting for the chasuble. He hesitated as long as possible and then he suddenly *leaped* toward me, thrust the chasuble at me, and jumped back to his previous position. It was quite a performance, and one that couldn't be missed by some of the choir, as I'm sure he intended. I had no suspicion that his bizarre behavior was part of a set-up that would later be revealed. In fact, I could never have imagined it.

There were other petty things he did in an attempt to make me a non-person as far as St. John's was concerned. At first, I didn't notice that my name had been removed from the service schedule for June. I didn't notice it because I was no longer receiving the service schedules and newsletter. Fr. Martin had removed my

---

3        A poncho-like vestment that can be simple cotton or a rich brocade fabric, heavily embroidered. Fr. Martin liked the elaborate ones.

name from the mailing list.

By that time, the only job I had left was Altar Guild, the one I loved most. When my team was on duty, I always did the altar flower arrangements on which I usually spent many hours in selecting the flowers, polishing the vases, and creating the two large matching arrangements for the altar, another small one for the Sunday school, a tiny one to put in the memorial window for Gaby's daughter, and a lapel flower for each usher. It was always a pleasure to do it and to see them on Sunday mornings. Mid-week, I normally set up the altar for Communion, and on Thursdays, I went to the outdoor market to buy the Sunday flowers, spending my own money.

I called Gaby on a Wednesday evening to confirm that I would be going to market the next day. Instead of her usual thanks for letting her know, there was a long silence that gave me a deep, sickening feeling. I knew what was coming and asked her, "He took me off the Altar Guild, didn't he?"

Gaby answered very quietly, "Yes."

It was difficult to continue talking, but I managed to ask her before I started crying, "When did you know?"

"Two weeks ago." She paused for a moment and I could tell that she, too, was upset. She then continued, "I wanted to tell you, but he wouldn't let me."

After I hung up, I spent the rest of the evening in heartbroken tears. On Sunday when I went to church, I wanted to cry all over again. The altar flowers were skimpy and poorly arranged. As I sat in my pew, I consoled myself by thinking, "Well, he's taken away everything now. There's nothing more he can do to me." But, I was wrong—*very* wrong. Unhappy and sad as I was over the way Fr. Martin had treated me, I resolved again that this time *I would not leave*. I knew that there were other people he had pushed out, but I would not be one of them.

After church one Sunday, Carole, who now frequently attended St. John's, asked Frank Reynolds, a respected senior member who was very close to Fr. Martin, "Why is Fr. Martin treating Rayn this way?" He answered in a very disapproving way, "She's made inappropriate advances toward him," without telling her what was meant by "inappropriate advances." He later told others that I had tried to lure Fr. Martin into my hot tub. Very few people even knew that I had a hot tub. I used it only by myself and occasionally offered it to a female house guest. It was never part of any social gathering or party, and I shared it only once—with Monica—when we had finished cleaning up after the February 28 dinner party. I had, however, offered it one time to Fr. Martin when we were still friends and I was completely ignorant of what he was saying behind my back, but it was nothing like what he later claimed.

After a Friday night banquet at the NPS, where drinks and wine are always served, Fr. Martin and his students, along with Scott Jackson and some of the other men, went to Lollapalooza, a popular Martini bar in downtown Monterey. Carole had taken me there for a drink on my birthday, and I can attest that the drinks are very good, but large and potent. One had been enough for me.

Fr. Martin phoned me the following afternoon, Saturday. He sounded awful and complained that he had a terrible hangover that was making it difficult for him to write his Sunday morning sermon. He explained that he'd gone to the dinner and the club the evening before. I was somewhat amused by his situation, but sympathetic for his predicament. He questioned how he could preach to others when he, himself, sometimes did the wrong thing. Trying to be helpful, I lightheartedly suggested that he think about something he *hadn't* done, and preach about that. The next day the sermon was as good as always, and no one would have suspected that he'd had such a hard time with it. He told me later that he'd resurrected an old one. I thought, well, we all believe in resurrection.

That same Sunday evening, Fr. Martin and Scott came

to my house for dinner. While we were standing around in the kitchen, chatting before dinner, Scott brought up the Friday night visit to Lollapalooza and told Fr. Martin that he should not have behaved as he had with two of the girls who were there. I couldn't imagine how he would have misbehaved with them, and when I asked Scott what had happened, he said that Fr. Martin gave them a lecture about the revealing way they were dressed, and it was more than just a passing comment or a few words. I thought it kind of funny because it was so very typical of Fr. Martin to criticize that sort of thing, but I had to agree with Scott that it was none of his business and he had no right to do it. They were probably dressed no differently than most of the other women. After all, the place attracts a young crowd and it was a typical Friday night in downtown Monterey.

Fr. Martin became very defensive, even a bit angry with our criticism, and he emphatically repeated that they shouldn't have been in the bar wearing such skimpy clothes. I thought, maybe he shouldn't have been in the bar wearing his collar—or even in the bar at all. He insisted that he was right, he'd done nothing wrong, and that was the end of the subject for the rest of the evening.

It turned out that one of the bartenders knew the girls and overheard the conversation with Fr. Martin. By Monday, a friend of mine had heard about the encounter and, knowing that I attended St. John's, told me that one of the girl's fathers was so angry at Fr. Martin's chastising the two girls that he called the bishop to complain. I thought to myself, that's going to lead to a little chat behind the wood shed.

Vestry meetings always started promptly at 7:00, but at the meeting on Tuesday, Fr. Martin was late, a very unusual occurrence. I hadn't seen or spoken to him since dinner on Sunday night and when he arrived, I was shocked at his appearance. He was slouched over and looked almost ill. He'd once told me that he'd had a nervous breakdown, and I feared that he was about to have another. I immediately thought he must have heard from the bishop—very harshly heard from the bishop—about his public behavior. We zipped through the agenda, and the meeting ended in record time. After the meeting, Fr. Martin was coming to my house for a Philly steak sandwich, and church talk. He had to first stop by his house for some papers, and he still appeared to be on the edge of a breakdown, so I suggested that he grab a swim suit while he was at home and he could get in the hot tub. It never entered my mind to join him, or that he might think that I would do so.

He phoned me from home, said he was exhausted and was heading straight to bed. That was the end of the hot tub story—I thought—and I never offered it to him on any other occasion, nor did I ever invite him to join me.

Fr. Martin would later tell a very different story when questioned under oath. He said, "I was made uncomfortable by the suggestions at times, and I confided in a few people about this with regard to maybe joining her in the hot tub. I mean that—at first, I sort of blew it off and thought well just, you know, deal with it, whatever. But then I thought—I don't know—it made me a little bit uncomfortable."

Asked how many times I had invited him to join me in the hot tub, Fr. Martin corrected the question to, "*Suggested* that I might like to join her in the hot tub," and then he answered, "Maybe five. Five or six" times as to when it started to make him uncomfortable, as he claimed. He said, "It was progress—it just made me uncomfortable progressively, and I didn't think it was appropriate." When asked what I was wearing when I'd supposedly made the suggestions, he answered that I was always fully dressed and not wearing a swimsuit.

# CHAPTER FIVE

# She That Believeth and Is Baptized
# Shall Be Saved

My belief that there was nothing more Fr. Martin could do to me did not last long. Not long at all, because on May 11, 2003, he announced that anyone who could not prove they had been baptized and confirmed in the Trinitarian tradition[4] would no longer receive Communion. The only exceptions were people who transferred from other Episcopal churches, or who had been members of St. John's for five years.

Fr. Martin knew I did not directly transfer from another Episcopal church and that I'd joined St. John's only *three* years earlier. When he wanted me elected to the vestry in 2001, I'd asked him if I could take that position, not having been baptized or confirmed in the Episcopal Church. His reply had been that of course I could; it made no difference. He'd treated it as a rather silly question.

I knew that I had been baptized in the Lutheran Church (Trinitarian) but didn't know in which specific church. I remembered my godparents' names, but both they and my birth parents were deceased. There was no one to ask. I went to Sunday school every week while growing up, and in the ninth grade I went to Catechism classes and was confirmed, as is the tradition in most Protestant churches.

I spent hours making long distance phone calls to inquire of the churches that were possibilities. Some had old baptism records, and some did not. Some had to check archives, and others

---

4    Belief in the Holy Trinity of Father, Son and Holy Spirit

didn't know what happened to their records. After exhausting every possibility, I called Fr. Wolter, the retired priest who had filled in while St. John's searched for a new priest. He said that if my mother hadn't offered proof of my baptism, I would not have been accepted into Catechism class, or been confirmed.

Luckily, I remembered the name of the church that confirmed me and I called them. A record search provided a partial list of names for our confirmation class, but my name wasn't on it. I thought that ended it for me until the woman mentioned that they had a group photograph and she would send me a copy. When I took the photo from its envelope—there I was!

I was relieved and overjoyed that I had the proof I needed. But, my relief was premature, and I should have known it wouldn't be that simple. The requirements changed each week until someone demanded a clarification, and Fr. Martin now said we had to provide proof of *baptism*. Confirmation alone would not be enough to receive Holy Communion and yet, Communion was offered to anyone seeking forgiveness of their sins. No person I spoke to ever heard of anyone, even visitors to churches where no one knew them—including ours—not being invited to participate. Condemned murders on their way to execution were offered Communion without proof of baptism, or even professing a belief in God!

One Sunday when Fr. Martin was exasperated over failure to comply with his demand for baptism proof, he shouted, "The Bishop is insisting!" Then he added in a sinister voice, "If you don't want to comply, perhaps you should leave the church." From that blunt and angry message, I knew my time was almost up. What's more, I knew that his anger and threat were intended for only me. But, there were magic words in that outburst, "The Bishop is insisting." If the bishop was insisting, that meant that all the other Episcopal Churches in our five-county, fifty-church diocese had to do the same thing. I called two local Episcopal churches and asked if they were under the same orders from the bishop. They didn't know what I was talking about. By now, that was not the least bit surprising to me, and when I explained it to them, they said they'd never heard of such a requirement and wouldn't even think of applying it to their congregations or anyone else who came to their churches. Now I knew for certain that it was not the bishop's demand, as Fr. Martin claimed. It was only his demand, and my belief that it was directed exclusively at me would later be confirmed.

On May 29, I wrote to Richard Schimpfky, the bishop of our diocese, and explained the problems I was having locating my baptism records, *as he'd requested*. I asked, "Why are the other Episcopal churches not doing likewise? Is it your position that those not complying should leave the church?" Bishop Shimpfky wrote in a June 4 letter to me, that it was important for churches to upgrade their records during the bi-centennial. This was three and a half years later! He said that if I submitted to a conditional baptism,[5] he "would be honored to come and be part of the act with you and your rector."

My rector! I would never consider asking the priest who'd lied about me and was doing everything he could think of to get rid of me, to perform my baptism. The thought of him baptizing me was absolutely repugnant. I'd let Satan do it before Fr. Martin. Not only that, but the implication was that it would have to be part of a regular Sunday church service. I couldn't imagine myself, a grown woman leaning over a baptism font in the presence of an entire congregation.

It was back to Fr. Wolter who suggested that I ask Fr. Jeff Kraemer, the rector of St. Dunstan's church in Carmel Valley, to privately baptize me. I wrote to him and hearing nothing back, I phoned to inquire if he'd received my letter. His secretary assured me that he had. I left a message with her, and another one after that, asking him to phone me. He never phoned or wrote.

---

5       When it is believed that a person was baptized but there is no proof of it, a conditional baptism can be performed so that the person is certain they have met that Christian requirement.

I knew that I had been baptized, and I knew that God welcomed me to Holy Communion, but the wheels against me kept turning—more than I could ever have imagined. And those wheels, I learned over three years later, were also intended only for me.

About two weeks after I had received the Bishop's letter supporting Fr. Martin, the bishop's secretary phoned to say that the bishop wished to see me, and she wanted to set the appointment immediately. By then, I trusted no one who wore a clerical collar, and my instincts were as tightly tuned and alert as an animal in the wild evading a hunter. I sensed what was coming, and it was not an invitation to tea.

I was cornered. A feeling of dread and panic rushed through me and I had to sit down, but I would not willingly lay my head on the block and gracefully accept the final blow. I told her "No." I said I did not want to meet with Bishop Shimpfky. Foolishly, I'd hoped that would end it, but in no more time than it would have taken to relay my answer to the bishop, she called again. With a stern, officious bluntness, she told me that when the Bishop wished to see someone, "no" was not an acceptable answer. A meeting was set for June 26.

CHAPTER SIX

# Thou Shalt

I'd never met Bishop Shimpfky and had seen him only once, when he'd paid an official Sunday visit to St. John's. Because I knew that Fr. Martin had lied and everyone had believed him, I wondered how I could trust the bishop. If there were a conflict about what we said, people would believe him, not me. If people thought that a priest wouldn't lie, they surely would never believe that a bishop would lie. I considered surreptitiously recording our conversation, but that would be dishonest, and I didn't know how to do it without the risk of being found out. If I asked permission, the answer would likely be no, and he would realize that I didn't trust him, so I asked Carole to go with me. I didn't tell him she would be joining us because if he knew ahead of time, he might insist that it be just the two of us.

Behind my back, as was his cowardly custom, Fr. Martin made certain that my credibility with the bishop would be destroyed before I even arrived for the meeting. He sent Bishop Shimpfky an email that preceded me, and that email is very likely what had led to the bishop summoning me to the diocese. I first learned of the email three years later. Fr. Martin wrote:

"Dear Bishop, I am going to drop a series of missives sent by this lady to me. She refuses to allow me to be a priest or rector. She has challenged my authority to remove her from the Flower Guild, and then the position of Treasurer of the Altar Guild. She has sent the letters to others.[6] She is neither a member of St. John's, nor is she an Episcopalian. I can have no right of appeal to my superiors or the institution of the church if she is not a member.

---

6    The people he, himself, originally copied

I know that this sounds legalistic, but I must have a role in the church vis-a-vis those who are more than visitors. I removed her from her positions for a few reasons. She had been harassing me, and then without consulting me, asked another lady to take over responsibilities with the flower guild. So I replaced her. Later I removed her as treasurer of the Altar Guild because, quite frankly, I did not want to have to deal with her on a personal basis any longer. She has been inappropriate with me. She has given off the wrong impression. We tried to involve her in our fellowship life, because she appeared as one who needed friends. She mistook this for another kind of love. She was wholly uninterested in our church family, and rather increasingly built up a relationship in her mind with me. She is old, and dresses like a trashy young woman. She refuses to acknowledge the role and responsibilities of the wardens. She threatens me in the final letter, as you will see. I need a letter from you, I think. I am sickened about giving her Communion. She should, at least, like all others, have to provide us with her Baptismal record if she wishes to participate even minimally. You alone, I think, can handle this one. Please help me. I am a sensitive person, I know. I hate to hurt people. But sometimes a cancer has to be removed. I shall drop off the letters."

It was signed, "Yours, Fr. Martin."

I can only imagine what kind of woman the bishop expected to see, and I could never have imagined that anyone would, or even could, create such a false and vile portrait of me. I walked into the bishop's office as a total innocent who had been summoned to appear before the person that William Martin hoped would be my spiritual executioner. When Bishop Shimpfky's secretary ushered Carole and me into his office, he greeted us cordially, and if his face reflected surprise at the two properly dressed and respectable women who had appeared, I didn't notice.

He wore his collar, but dressed casually in a sport coat and slacks. He seemed to be about 60 years old, more or less, and there was nothing distinctive about him that would attract anyone's attention. When I introduced Carole and told him that she could hear anything that either of us said, he made no objection.

I, unknowingly, gave him copies of the very same letters he had received from Fr. Martin, and we talked for more than an hour as I related the background, the events, and my concerns about where I stood in the church. As the conversation progressed, I felt increasingly certain that I was not what he had expected, and I also sensed that he hadn't anticipated what I had to tell him, which was confirmed by Carole. When I'd finished speaking, he momentarily looked at me without saying anything, as though he first had to let everything sink in. When he finally spoke, he asked in a kindly, almost apologetic voice, "Rayn, what do you want?"

I immediately said, "I want an apology from Fr. Martin for the lies he has told about me. It should be from the pulpit because lies publicly told should be publicly redressed, but I know that will never happen. So, I want it in writing, because if it isn't in writing, he'll deny it. I want to know that I will never be denied Communion and that I will never be asked to leave St. John's."

His only answer was, "That can be done."

After I returned home, I sent a letter to Bishop Shimpfky thanking him and confirming the three things he'd promised me. I said that because the damage done to my reputation was so widespread, Fr. Martin should inform the Vestry and the ECW that he apologized to me. Even if that embarrassed and humiliated him, it didn't come close to the embarrassment and humiliation he had caused me. I thanked the bishop again for his empathy, understanding, and faithfulness to the Office of Bishop, and I even suggested that the Roman Catholic bishops could take a lesson from him.

He sent a hand-written note on his personal stationery with the Diocese crest that assured me:

"Dear Rayn, I have your letter. Rectors in our tradition don't apologize in these (illegible)." The words "don't apologize" stopped me right there. If parishioners confessd their sins and asked God's forgiveness, it seemed to me that a priest ought to be able to at least apologize for a wrongdoing. Shimpfky was protecting Fr. Martin again, as he had with his bi-centennial excuse for Martin's baptism demands. The note continued, "Your place, meanwhile at St. John's, and at Communion is secure." He signed it, "Blessings, Richard," and drew a small cross above his name.

Denial of the apology was hurtful. It was the first thing I'd asked for, and if Fr. Martin had apologized, my other requests would have been unnecessary. Bishop Shimpfky had the authority to demand that Fr. Martin apologize, and he had the power to discipline him, even remove him. Nevertheless, I believed I could trust Bishop Shimpfky's word—in his own handwriting—and Fr. Martin could no longer harm me or force me to leave St. John's. I felt that I had been fairly treated and would be in the future.

I continued to attend services every Sunday—baptism was never once mentioned again—and I received Communion with just a tiny twist. Prior to my visit with the bishop, Fr. Martin had shown his hateful feelings for me by the way he gave me the Communion wafer. Instead of firmly placing it in my hand as is customary, he would hold it above my hands and then let go, so it would fall. I knew how he felt about me, but the wafer represents the body of Christ. It was shocking disrespect coming from an ordained disciple of Christ. I'd mentioned this to Bishop Shimpfky and now Fr. Martin no longer did that. Instead, he put the wafer in my hand very carefully so as not to accidentally touch me, and then he would quickly withdraw his hand as though he might be burned.

Someone asked me how I could continue to accept Communion from him, and I answered that he was only a delivery system. That's exactly how I saw him. For me, there was no longer anything spiritual about him, and I was more determined than ever that he was not going to drive me from my church. I knew enough about the man who was supposed to be our spiritual leader that I no longer respected him. But, if I let him drive me away, I would have even less respect for myself.

I didn't want to shake his hand, or even speak to him on the way out of church, but it was impossible to avoid it without being obvious. It would also be noticed by everyone if I slipped out the little side door by the wheelchair ramp instead of the main door, as I always had. People would ask why, and having learned my lesson about congregation suspicion and speculation, I wanted to avoid it. To solve the problem, I took the left arm of my dear, elderly, and frail pew mate, Bob Hickcox, to assist him when we got to the top of the outside steps where Fr. Martin always stood. Bob's right hand was free to take Fr. Martin's hand, and they exchanged pleasantries while I stood on the far side. No one, not even Bob, noticed that I never spoke.

Fr. Martin had made his feelings about me—that he didn't want me there—clear to the ECW members, and many of them didn't hesitate to show their dislike for my presence, so I stopped attending the luncheon meetings. However, a new acquaintance, Dorothy Finell, whom I'd met at a Salvation Army fundraiser, wrote a book about her very interesting Jewish family history, and she was invited to speak about it at an ECW luncheon. She didn't know any of the women and asked me for my moral support, so I promised to attend, even though I knew I would not be welcomed.

When I entered the church hall where the luncheon was held, I immediately felt an undeniable chill. No one greeted me and no one invited me to sit next to her. Cold glares, one of them from the president who was seated at the head table next to Dorothy, were thrown my way like sharp knives. I hadn't expected it to be quite that bad and didn't know which way to move or where to sit until Pat Vince, a part-time member from Canada, stood and called me over to her table. Even the women who had been my friends were barely polite, and it was obvious that it was forced only by an instinct for good manners. I knew it was Fr. Martin at work, so I wasn't surprised, but I was emotionally crushed and helpless to present any defense. I didn't even know what I had to defend myself from. They were called the Episcopal Church Women, but by that time, Fr. Martin controlled them so completely that they should have changed their name to FMECW—Fr. Martin's Episcopal Church Women.

Jo Howard said the following when asked how I was treated by others when she and I first met: "Rayn was a very quiet lady. She would always speak to people, and they spoke to her. They were friendly." Asked how that changed, she answered, "In 2003, some people began to treat her like she had the plague. At coffee, people just turned, or went away. I remember thinking I didn't know how she was doing that."

Then she was asked, "What happened when Rayn walked into ECW meetings?" Jo answered, "There were two or three occasions. We would be talking, serving lunch and things would be going on. And, suddenly, when Rayn would come in, it would be dead silence. It would just get very quiet. And, I don't remember anybody greeting her."

Around this same time there was a crisis within the National Episcopal Church USA—ECUSA—headquartered in New York. In an October, 2003, issue of a local newspaper, *The Coast Weekly*, the cover photo and main story were about the rapidly widening schism between the national church and many parishes throughout the US. The conflict was caused by the installation of an openly gay, non-celibate priest, Vicki Gene Robinson, as Bishop of New Hampshire. The new bishop lived with his lover,[7] in a house they had purchased together, and their union was celebrated by many, including ECUSA and the then Presiding Bishop, Frank Griswold. The paper featured a long article about St. John's that included several photos. The heading read:

"A Monterey minister leads his flock back to the 1920s— When God was tough, gays were sinners, and women knew their place."

---

7        They were joined in a civil union in June of 2008, followed by an Episcopal Church blessing. Robinson had earlier said that he always wanted to be a June Bride.

It quoted notes that Fr. Martin had written for an August sermon:

"It should come as no surprise to anyone that the Episcopal Church of the United States of America has enthusiastically elected its first openly homosexual Bishop. The latest decision taken by the church's voting members to the General Convention is the result of a chronic spiritual disease.

"We at St. John's reject and repudiate the actions taken by General Convention. We deplore the pride and arrogance of silly churches who parade around claiming to sell spiritual wares in the shop at Vanity Fair.

"From a traditional Christian standpoint, the new Church's dependence and reliance upon the world is truly sinful. What used to be maintained as sinful behaviour is now promoted as virtuous and noble."

The article goes on, "Writing to the *Weekly* in an email from an abbey in France, where he spent the past two weeks, Martin levels harsh judgment against his colleagues. Martin warns that St. John's will not submit to 'Baal,' the pagan idol whose worship was most often excoriated by the ancient Hebrew prophets."

He is later quoted, "God becomes a tool of our fancies and imaginations. And in the end, God is really non-existent. The self sees the self, and there you have it—spiritual masturbation."
Frank Reynolds was asked about gays and he said, "It's not like we have a big sign on the door that says, 'No homosexuals.'"[8]

Fr. Martin said, "When I got here, there were a few bigoted people. I said, No, no, no, what about your own lives? What's in your closet?"

It's a question he might appropriately have asked himself.

---

8     The church organist/music director, Clay Couri, is a homosexual man who for many years has lived openly with his gay partner. Fr. Martin disparaged them to me, but was a frequent guest at their home. Clay is an outstanding chef and I once also had dinner at their home when Fr. Martin was present.

# CHAPTER SEVEN

# Of That Day and That Hour, Knoweth No Man....Or Woman

In 2004, Ash Wednesday came on February 25. In Christian churches, Ash Wednesday marks the beginning of Lent, a six-week period of repentance in preparation for the joyful celebration of Christ's Resurrection on Easter Sunday—the very foundation of Christianity. St. John's observed that day with a simple two part service that had no music and no sermon. In the first part, Fr. Martin placed a cross mark, made from the prior year's palm ashes mixed with oil, on participants' foreheads as they knelt at the altar rail. That was followed by a second trip to the altar for Holy Communion.

At St. John's there was room for eight people at the Communion rail. Approaching from the center aisle, the first four turned right and the next four turned left. All would kneel together, and after everyone received the Communion wafer, followed separately by the wine, they all stood up and exited to their right as the next eight people stepped up to take their places. Everyone returned to their seats via the side aisle, two steps down from the altar level. On Sunday mornings there was always someone to assist people so that no one tripped on the carpeted stairs, but at mid-week services, no one was there.

Bob didn't come that morning, and I sat alone in our usual pew. On the first trip to the altar for the ashes—I was the first person in that group—I felt Fr. Martin make the sign of the cross on my forehead and heard him say, "Dust thou art, and to dust thou shalt return."

When I later approached the altar for Communion, I was again, the first person, so I went to the far right where the priest always began his progression down the line of parishioners. I was on my knees, my arms resting on the altar rail, and my hands held open in front of me to receive the Communion wafer. Fr. Martin did not give me one. He started with the man on my left.

I knew instantly that it was intentional, but couldn't believe it. I tried to tell myself that he wouldn't dare defy the bishop's promise to me; maybe he made a mistake. He kept his eyes closed a lot during Communion. Perhaps he just hadn't seen me, or he wasn't paying attention. I watched him out of the corner of my eye as he went down the line giving a wafer to each person while saying, "This is the body of Christ…" I kept my hands open in front of me, thinking he might have second thoughts and come back to me. He didn't.

I watched as he put down the silver wafer bowl and picked up the chalice of wine that he had blessed. He turned back to us, paused, and offered it to the man next to me saying, "This is Christ's blood…" and then proceeded down the row. This time, I couldn't bear to watch. After he'd finished and set the chalice back on the credence table, he turned back to us again and stood directly in front of me, only inches away. My eyes were on his shoes. The hem of his cassock lifted slightly as he raised his hand in a blessing, and then I watched the shoes turn away. That was the sign for us to stand and leave. *Fr. Martin had denied me Communion.*

I had to stand up. I had to be the first person to move. But, I didn't have the strength to get up from my knees. My entire body was drained, it felt as though every muscle had liquefied, and my brain no longer had enough oxygen to keep it functioning because I could barely breathe. Everyone was already standing and waiting for me. Finally, I put my hands on the altar rail and summoned enough strength to push myself to my feet. When I turned toward the steps, my head was spinning and my eyes filled with tears so quickly that the steps became a blur and I couldn't tell where they began. Memory of habit came to me as I cautiously stepped down without falling. I had to walk all the way to the back of the church to get to my pew which was on the other side. My legs felt so weak that I thought my knees would collapse and I'd never make it, but I had to. I *had* to keep walking or I would dissolve into the floor. On the wall facing me at the end of the long aisle, there was a small cross, and I kept my eyes focused on it, without looking down or to the side. I felt as though I were walking a narrow ledge on a tall building, and if I made one misstep, or looked down, I would die.

When I got back to my pew, I started trembling, and my heart was pounding so hard that I had to fight my body to make it stop. The service ended, and I wanted to escape before the people near the front of the church got back to me. I don't remember leaving, but I got to my car. Once inside, I completely broke down in a state of shock that I couldn't control.

I heard the few other cars as they drove away, but I didn't dare try to drive. I was alone in the parking lot. I couldn't stop shaking, and I couldn't stop crying.

At last, my hands stopped trembling enough for me to take out my cell phone and call Carole. She was in a meeting, but thankfully, she answered her phone. I told her what Fr. Martin had done and started to sob all over again. She couldn't leave the meeting, but she stayed on the phone and talked to me until I was collected enough to drive home. I don't remember the drive either, only the focused, intense knowledge that I had to get there before I lost it again. I had to get to the only safe place that remained for me.

After many more tears, I thought very hard about whether I could handle the torment I was getting from Fr. Martin, and I had to decide what I would do about it. In a day or two, when I felt stronger, I resolved once again that I would not leave St. John's. I'd done nothing wrong, and when I got my thoughts back in order, I would meet with Bishop Shimpfky. He would keep his word to me, and Fr. Martin would never again dare to deny me Communion.

Bob wasn't at church the next Sunday so, to avoid Fr. Martin, I left by the little side door handicap ramp. I saw Martha—the woman for whom we'd had the birthday dinner—who always used that door, and we walked out together. It was a beautiful, warm, sunny day, and we paused to chat on the pathway that went through our small rose garden.

While we were talking, a tall and stern looking older man abruptly appeared next to me and introduced himself as Howard Sitton, the Senior Warden. He addressed me as "Miss Random" and flatly stated that Fr. Martin wanted me to leave. Martha and I were dumbfounded by his demand, so he repeated it. He said that Fr. Martin wanted to pass by where we were standing, and I had to leave so that he could. It was ridiculous because Fr. Martin never used the side handicap door or came anywhere near that area. For a moment, I tried to understand the why of the man's demand and when I didn't immediately leave, his demeanor turned threatening and I thought he was going to grab me to physically remove me. Martha later told me that she thought the same thing.

Behind him, I glimpsed a woman whom I assumed was Mrs. Sitton, standing nearby. She was a large woman, plain looking and smugly righteous appearing, somewhat like the sour-faced woman in Grant Woods' painting, *American Gothic*. She was watching us intently, and when I looked directly at her, she lifted her chin and gave me a contemptuous, holier-than-thou smile as if I were some disgusting and vile woman who was getting exactly what she deserved, and she appeared proud that it was her husband who was seeing to my riddance. I couldn't understand why this was happening. It was Kafkaesque.

I thought Warden Sitton meant that I should leave that particular spot, not the entire church premises, so I suggested to Martha that we go for coffee. During the time I was in the parish hall, he kept his eyes laser-focused on me as though he were a

Secret Service Agent guarding the president in a dangerous third world country. I half expected him to physically force me out, but there were too many witnesses who might be horrified at the sight.

Mr. Sitton wrote a later revealed memorandum to Fr. Martin about that morning wherein he said that he feared I would physically confront Fr. Martin, and if Fr. Martin entered the room, he (Sitton) would be sure to keep *his own body* between Fr. Martin and me. The idea was absurd, and I could only conclude that Mr. Sitton nurtured a hero fantasy. There were many more strange attitudes among the congregation that I had yet to discover.

The next day, Monday, I had a lunch date in Carmel with Dorothy Finell. Although weeks earlier she'd asked me to be at the ECW luncheon, we didn't know each other well and were meeting to become better acquainted. While we waited for our lunch to be served, she described a dinner party that she'd attended the night before with two Arab students she sponsored from the NPS. Dorothy thought it a small contribution to international understanding and friendship for a Jewish woman to sponsor Arab students.

Very little understanding occurred that evening because the host chose to talk about the new film, "Passion of the Christ." While everyone was still seated at the table after they had finished the main course, he launched into a tirade of anti-Jewish sentiments to the point that Dorothy chose to skip dessert and depart with her students in spite of his anxious pleadings that they return to the table. I knew it had to be Fr. Martin—Dorothy had only met the ECW woman when she spoke at St. Johns—and when I said his name and told her that he was the priest at St. John's, she could hardly believe it.

After relating Fr. Martin's anti-Jewish outburst at the Author's Table dinner, I told her about his denying me Communion and my being asked to leave the church property only the day before. The timing of our lunch date was an astonishing coincidence, but

Dorothy had an even more appaling surprise for me. She said that Fr. Martin announced to all of his guests that *a woman at his church was stalking him*. I knew immediately who that woman was supposed to be—me.

My lunch with Dorothy was on March 8 of 2004. I found out nine months later, in December, that Fr. Martin had been spreading that lie both within and outside of the church for almost two years. His behavior at the back of the church when he practically threw the chasuble at me and acted so frightened of me must have been his dramatic debut performance to substantiate that accusation. Again, no one ever told me or questioned me about it, and I never suspected he could do such a vile thing—to *anyone*.

On Wednesday of that week, March 10, I phoned Bishop Shimpfky's office requesting a meeting with him. While I waited for a call back, I began a letter to him describing what had happened on Ash Wednesday and on Sunday. I was half way through the letter when his secretary phoned to tell me that Bishop Shimpfky had refused to see me. I couldn't believe it. He'd given me his word and now he wouldn't even speak with me. I was being more and more isolated. It was a terrible, crushing feeling, almost as though I were being squeezed until I suffocated, and I didn't know where to turn. I don't recall anything particular about Thursday except for the sadness and despair that I felt, but I will never forget Friday.

In the morning, I took care of my dogs and my cat as always, but there was nothing on my mind except the bewilderment of why this was happening. Why would William Martin do this to me? Why did Bishop Shimpfky not keep his word? My dogs heard someone coming up my driveway and began to bark, interrupting my thoughts and jolting me back to the present. When I went outside to investigate, a man I'd never seen was standing at the wrought iron gate, and after I confirmed to him that I was Rayn Random, he thrust a letter at me through the gate. It was from the

St. John's Vestry. I knew I'd better sit down before I read it, so I took it into the house. The vestry had written:

"Dear Ms. Random:

The purpose of this letter is to inform you that the Rector, Vestry and Wardens of St. John's Chapel, Del Monte, no longer wish to see you on St. John's Chapel property and consider any further presence by you on that property to be trespassing."

They said that I was not a "respectful parishioner, anxious to enhance all congregants' quiet, tranquil contemplation of the meaning of their religious faith in their lives, but rather to interfere with that peaceful activity via bellicose letters or conduct." The letter was signed by nine members of the Vestry.

The outrageous and false accusations were incomprehensible. I was too hurt and frustrated to think clearly or to decide what I should, or even *could,* do. It didn't matter, because the next day, Saturday, I found the following letter in my mailbox:

"Ms. Random:

"The Rector of St. John's Chapel, Del Monte acted in accord with the canons of the Church in denying you Communion, and I do not second guess the judgment of my clergy, especially so fine a priest as William Martin. Rayn, it is time for you to find another church to attend, and I wish you god speed in your search."

It was signed, The Rt. Rev. Richard L. Shimpfky and, of course—being a fine man of God, himself—he drew a little cross in the loop of the "R" on Richard.

It was over, and I had lost.

# CHAPTER EIGHT

# Revelation

Nineteen days after excommunicating me, Richard Shimpfky resigned as bishop of El Camino Real Diocese. Prior to that, he had taken a leave of absence due to "personal problems and depression." The Standing Committee of the diocese—a body of overseers similar to the vestry members of a church—had brought ecclesiastical charges against him. The charges were rejected on a technicality by the national Episcopal Church (ECUSA), but the diocese Standing Committee[9] refused to give up its pursuit of charges, and Shimpfky resigned. We had no bishop for nine months.[10] The Anglican web site, VirtueOnLine, reported that at one time, under Shimpfky's leadership, "Things deteriorated so badly that a priest yelled, 'You're a liar!' at him (Shimpfky) during a meeting."

I could have loudly shouted the very same thing at Bishop Shimpfky. I was told sometime later that Fr. Martin had defended Shimpfky prior to his resignation, and I suspect that excommunicating me was a parting favor of thanks to Fr. Martin. After all, Shimpfky would be leaving Monterey, and there would be nothing I could contest or hold him responsible for, as he was already being forced to resign.

At the time, however, my biggest question was, why did the vestry take such drastic action against me? What on God's earth had Fr. Martin told them—presumably God-fearing, respectable, Christian people—that they would charge me, judge me, condemn

9      A permanent committee that provides guidance to the diocese.
10     In December of that year, Sylvester Romero, from Belize, was appointed Acting Bishop. It took three more years to find and elect a new permanent bishop, the Rt. Rev. Mary Gray-Reeves, who was consecrated in November 2008.

me, and punish me by driving me from my church based only on what he had claimed. Had William Martin become Jim Jones in the Guyana jungle, and they had all drunk the poisoned Kool Aid?[11]

At my request, Pat Vince asked one of the vestry members who had signed the letter to me, why they had banished me. The man, who had once been a dinner guest in my home, slowly shook his head and said with great sympathy and sadness, "I felt so sorry for poor Fr. Martin." That's all he had to say, and Pat didn't inquire further.

In April, I had a conversation with a Naval Postgraduate School student sponsor whom I had met previously at Fr. Martin's house, and who had also been a guest at the last dinner party at my house. Much earlier, we had taken an instant liking to each other when we'd met at Fr. Martin's, and we occasionally got together for an after work drink to stay in touch. When I told her that Fr. Martin had denied me Holy Communion, she couldn't believe it. As a practicing Catholic, she was appalled, even somewhat outraged at the very idea and had never heard of any priest doing such a thing.

She then revealed that after we had met once before, she happened to mention our meeting to Fr. Martin in an unrelated phone call and his response had been explosive. He yelled at her, "How can you even speak to her after all the things I've told you about her?" Despite holding the phone at arm's length from her ear, not only could she still hear what he was shouting, but people seated nearby heard it, too. From this same woman, I learned for the first time that Fr. Martin had told her and others that I constantly phoned him, to the point that he had been forced to change his phone number.

It came as a surprise and a sad revelation to me that he had been spreading *this* lie for an entire year—while I was still at St. John's. Again, no one had told me.

---

11        It was not really Kool Aid, but that was the first report.

Of all the lies, the most horrifying was his accusation that I was stalking him. That claim had been running rampant as early as 2003, and aside from the devastating social consequences of being labeled a "stalker," it's a *crime punishable by imprisonment.* Under the (State of California) Penal Code Section 646.9, "a *first time* convicted stalker can be sentenced up to three years in state prison, even if there is no restraining order in effect." The Penal Code also provides that, "the sentencing court may issue a restraining order against the defendant that is valid for up to ten years, require that the stalker participate in counseling and, in certain cases, register as a *sex offender.* The court may also order that the defendant receive mental health treatment while incarcerated."

Anita Steel, a St. John's parishioner for over thirty years, testified that she first heard Fr. Martin claim that I was stalking him at a 2003 Christmas Party. She added, "I had many conversations with Fr. Martin (about Rayn Random), because he would call me in the middle of the night to complain that she was bothering him."

As to the vestry claim that I disturbed the congregation, Ms. Steel testified: "I have to tell you that Rayn Random in no way ever disrupted any congregation. She came, sat down, never spoke a word, took Communion, and left."

Jo Howard also testified that Fr. Martin had talked to her about my supposed stalking. She testified to the gist of their conversation, "Rayn Random was stalking him, that she was not quitting. She was calling him." Jo said that when she first heard that accusation, she had believed it because at the time, she had no reason not to, as Fr. Martin had turned us against each other.

When asked whether Fr. Martin ever said anything about my making inappropriate advances toward him, she replied, "It might have been July, August of 2003. This particular time, he was in London. And I, of course, was in Monterey. He telephoned and was very upset on the other end of the phone. He said that he had been sick, but that he had called his house and there were these lurid messages from Rayn Random on his telephone."

Sadly for me, Fr. Martin's lies not only caused me to lose my church, but they had a profound effect on people I had previously considered my friends. Adrianne always had a Christmas party in December and had reminded me several times prior to the 2004 party to be sure and save the date. Just before the party, she phoned and gave me a story about changing the date—she didn't tell me the new one—that resulted in my being uninvited. It was almost the same situation as Scott Jackson's wedding, but this time I instinctively knew the reason. Fr. Martin was also invited. Carole asked Clifford Bagwell, their mutual friend, to inquire of Adrianne why I wasn't coming. Adrianne told him, "She's *still* stalking Fr. Martin and, he has a restraining order against her." Without bothering to ask me if it was true, she had passed the lie on to Clifford. I was devastated. She was a friend, we'd had lunch together, we'd visited each others homes, and we saw each other frequently at church and charity fund raisers. After that, she blatantly snubbed me in public at every opportunity.

Fr. Martin's claim that he had a restraining order against me was a charge that could have been checked by anyone with a computer or a phone. It's a matter of public record at the court and any nearby police department. Getting a restraining order against someone is not a simple procedure. It requires convincing a judge to issue a temporary restraining order, then personal service of a Summons on the person to be restrained, and a court hearing in which both parties present evidence for and against making the temporary Order of Restraint permanent. If that had come to pass, Fr. Martin would have had to prove all his false claims before a judge, which he could not have done, and which I could have, and would have, refuted. No restraining order ever existed, nor was one ever sought by him. He would have had to expose himself as a liar right then and there.

During the time Fr. Martin and I were still friends, he began making disparaging comments to me about Jo and Dale Howard. At first the comments were insignificant and petty, but when the Howards and I became better acquainted, the comments became more critical and frequent until he finally told me to stay away from them and not to talk to them. He often repeated the admonition in a way that made it sound as though it was out of his concern for me. I was very disappointed by his warning because Jo and Dale had come to two of my dinner parties, and I liked them very much. But, I trusted Fr. Martin at that time and did as he said.

The most surprising thing that I heard him say was on one occasion when Jo and Dale were helping to prepare a meal for the entire congregation. They, Jo and Dale, were in the church kitchen until midnight, browning beef for a dish that Fr. Martin would finish the next day. The meat he'd provided had so much fat and gristle that it cooked down to much less than expected. But, Fr. Martin told me that there was less because they had "stolen" some of it. He warned me again not to talk with them.

When I had bought several roasts for the last dinner party that we hosted together—February 28, 2003—my refrigerator was crammed, and I wanted to store the roasts in one of the church refrigerators. Fr. Martin immediately said, "No! Don't do that! The Howards will steal them." It was becoming too much to believe, but I was very busy at the time with the party and didn't want to question or argue with him.

My banishment from the church coincided with Jo and Dale preparing to move to the East. By that time, I'd dismissed all of Fr. Martin's comments about other people, and I asked the Howards to stop by before they left. When they came to my house and we had a chance to talk, we realized that it was Fr. Martin who had destroyed our friendship. Just as he had admonished me to stay away from them, he had admonished them to stay away from me. He had good reason—he didn't dare risk our getting together and comparing notes.

Perhaps the most underhanded betrayal of his friendship with Jo and Dale occurred at the time of the Jackson wedding. The Howards had a son who lived near the wedding venue in Texas, and as a favor to his parents, he invited Fr. Martin to stay in his guest house. When Fr. Martin returned from the wedding, I was still unaware of why I'd been crossed off the guest list, and we were still on speaking terms. He told me that Jo and Dale's children had said they didn't even recognize their own mother anymore because she'd had so much plastic surgery.

Jo has never had cosmetic surgery, and none of her children ever made such a statement. During all the time that Fr. Martin lied to me about Jo and Dale, he accepted their hospitality and pretended to be their friend—just as he had done with me.

After my excommunication, I wasn't sure if I even wanted to find another church. All Saints in Carmel used the "new" 1978 version of *The Book of Common Prayer*, and the Sunday service was very different from the one I was familiar with. Their rector, Fr. Carl Hansen, was a welcoming and approachable man who had met with me after Fr. Martin denied me Communion. Fr. Hansen said he'd never encountered a similar situation, nor denied Communion to anyone. He was sympathetic, but there was nothing he could do to help me because we had no bishop at that time. He assured me that I was welcome at All Saints, and he gave me his blessing along with his cell phone number, telling me to call him whenever I needed to.[12]

When Easter Sunday approached, a good friend, Betty Meyer, asked me to accompany her for Easter service at St. Dunstan's Episcopal Church in Carmel Valley. The Rector was Fr. Jeff Kraemer, the same priest who had ignored me previously when I'd requested a private baptism. I joined her for Easter Sunday and then attended two more services there, each time feeling increasingly detached—because I was. During the last Sunday

---

12      I later heard a rumor that Fr. Hansen might be chosen to replace Bishop Shimpfky, and I rejoiced at the thought, but the rumor turned out to be untrue.

that I attended, one of the small children sitting with his parents had a big rag doll named "Jesus" that went home with a different child each week. I remembered when my son had brought home the kindergarten pet rat on weekends, and I wondered if these children were old enough to understand the difference between Jesus and a pet, or a toy. When the child who'd had "Jesus" with him the previous week, was asked what "Jesus" did during that time, the child had nothing to say. When Fr. Kraemer asked who wanted to take "Jesus" home for the coming week, there were no volunteers. It seemed like a well-intentioned idea, but more appropriate for Sunday school. To me, it was totally out of place in a church service for adults, and it left me wondering if that's what Jesus had been reduced to—a rag doll.

Fr. Kraemer greeted me after the service, but he appeared to not recognize my name, or that I'd asked him to baptize me, although I suspect that my excommunication was common knowledge along the local Episcopalian clergy grapevine. At coffee, Betty introduced me to another parishioner, and when Betty told her that I was from St. John's, the woman burst into gushing smiles and said, "Oh, we just *love* Fr. Martin!" She thought he was wonderful and proudly proclaimed that he was a frequent guest at her parties. She was looking straight at me with such anticipating delight, that I forced the expected smile. But, when she giddily said that they were trying to find a wife for him, I had to bite both of my lips to keep from laughing out loud, and I didn't have the heart to tell her she was on a futile search.

A few weeks later, I drove to the Carmel Mission, one of the Catholic churches built along historic El Camino Real in the 1700s by the Spanish—or, more accurately—by the labor of indigenous American Indians under the harsh rule of the Spaniards. Thinking that it might be more like St. John's because the Episcopal Church in the United States derives from The Anglican Church of England which, in turn, was originally Roman Catholic until King Henry VIII wanted to divorce Catherine of Aragon and marry Ann

Boleyn, I stepped inside for awhile.

The mission, beautiful and spiritual as it appears, didn't feel like the right place for me either, so I stopped going to any church. My faith and belief in God had not diminished or changed, but my view of the Episcopal Church and all churches was changed— forever.

Months had passed since I'd been forced out of St. John's, but on Sunday mornings whenever I looked at the time, I was reminded of what I used to be doing at that particular hour. A mist of sadness enveloped me, and I could not escape it, even with forced determination. I felt as though I was guilty of something, even though I knew I wasn't.

People outside of St. John's began to snub me. When I attended events, one or more people that I knew—even others that I *didn't* know—would deliberately turn away as I entered a room. In group conversations, someone would talk past me as though I were invisible. If I spoke, that person would deliberately speak over me to the person next to me.

One day I was at Orchard Supply Hardware and passed by David Jones, a member of St. John's who often served as an acolyte. Although I didn't know him personally, I'd always liked David because he'd always spoken to me in a pleasant manner. But that day in Orchard, he barely managed a curt, "Hello, Rayn," the tone of his voice filled with disgust. The contemptuous look on his face said, "Everyone knows what trash you are." The hurt was devastating.

At Staples, when I saw Kim Rennick from St. John's, I kept my face averted, hoping that she wouldn't see me, but then I heard her call out my name and I couldn't avoid talking to her. In later testimony, she was asked to describe our conversation and she recalled, "I walked up to her, and said, 'What's wrong, are you mad at me?' and she said, 'No'. She said 'I thought you wouldn't want to have anything to do with me because I—everybody is blackballing me, and saying I am a horrible person.'"

Although Kim had answered the church attorney's question, he became impatient and demanded, "What I want to know is what Ms. Random said to you about Fr. Martin—let me finish! Okay? What did *she* say—beyond what you've already told me?" Kim, who always spoke truthfully and thoroughly, needed no pushing from him to complete her answer. Her patient reply was, "She didn't," and Kim then restated her original response. That would not be the only time that attorney Swartz got angry when he didn't get what he wanted and took out his frustration on her. Kim had stood out as a rare bright light in the darkness of my social encounters.

The first Christmas after my excommunication, while I was at a Carmel art gallery party, I was introduced to Walter Alsky. He is now my friend, but at that time he still believed the things Fr. Martin had directly told him about me. In his pre-trial deposition, Walter was asked, "When you first met Rayn Random at the art gallery, did you speak with her at all?"

Walter answered, "No. I was told she was introduced and I—this I don't recall, but I was told—'you walked away from her.'" Walter also talked about another occasion when we had been in the same room. He said, "There is a Thursday once-a-month dance out Carmel Valley Road with an orchestra, and we were with our little group, dance group, and there was Rayn. And I said to myself what the hell is *she* doing here."

My attorney asked, "Why did you say that to yourself?"

Walter replied, "After all I heard about her, you know, I just thought, what is *she* doing here with us? You know? She was in our—going to be in our group."

When asked if he had ever heard William Martin say anything about me, Walter answered, "Oh, yes. Yes. That she was harassing him, phoning him, constantly in his way. And Martin told me that she used to sit in the front pew and goo-goo eye up at him. And the first time, I have to say this, when I went to church with Rayn, I started up to the front row, and she said 'where are you going?' And I said you always sit in the front row. And she said, 'No, I sit in the third row from the rear.' So we sat in the third row from the rear."

On the same subject of my behavior in church, my attorney asked Clifford, "Did you ever have a conversation with the church's organist about how Rayn Random behaved in church?"

"Oh, yes," Clifford replied, "Clay Couri, at his home. He said, 'Rayn Random comes to church, prances down the aisle, dressed with her boobs showing almost as if'—not boobs, tits is what he said—'almost like they are going to pop out.'"

I had always been nice to Clay at church, and complimented his brilliant organ performances many times. It was especially stunning to hear that even he had attacked me so cruelly—and falsely.

As the social rejections continued, the emotional toll on my health and mental state was increasing. Whenever I met someone new, I felt more anguish than pleasure. My first thoughts were always whether this person had heard what Fr. Martin had said? Was his or her smile genuine, or concealing disgust? I couldn't very well say to the person, "I'm not the terrible woman you may have heard about. None of those things is true." I could only wonder, and the stress of constantly wondering was debilitating.

Finally, I just tried to avoid people so as not to expose myself to more pain. I seldom felt like attending the numerous social or charity events that I had once enjoyed, and when I did, I mentally steeled myself for what I might encounter. I was so afraid of contributing to anyone's idea that I was the disreputable town stalker in scandalous pursuit of an innocent priest, that I even began dressing differently, wearing mostly black. I fell into the habit of looking in the mirror to make sure my skirt was long enough, my heels weren't too high. I decided my hair, naturally blonde, was too light, and I asked my hairdresser to make it a darker color.

To my surprise, I was asked to join the board of an

organization that I especially liked and supported. I immediately assumed that the person who asked me hadn't heard what was being said about me. When I'd had no contact from the organization for several weeks, I assumed that the other board members had probably been horrified at what she'd done and didn't want to have me associated with them. Happily, it turned out I'd been mistaken, but that was my state of mind at that time.

I'd been told by my few remaining friends, who knew better than I what was being said about me, that I had to stop Fr. Martin's endless slander. They insisted that my decision to do nothing in the belief that he would tire of it and give up talking about me, was wrong. Nine months had passed since I'd been excommunicated and forced from St. John's, but he still continued to slander me at every opportunity. Clifford told me that my doing nothing was making his lies more believable, and they were getting worse and spreading farther. It had become clear that Fr. Martin would never quit until he was forced to, and everywhere he went, my reputation was dragged along under his feet, becoming more and more soiled and tattered. I had become party entertainment.

Being stalked by a woman, a woman who was—or at least had been—a respected member of the community, gave Martin attention, sympathy, and a certain cachet that made him even more popular. It made him more attractive and exciting as a man, and not just any man, but a man of *God*. It made him everything to everyone, except me, because I knew that he was a man who neither deserved respect, nor was devoted to God.

There was no longer any doubt in my mind as to what I had to do after the 2004 holidays were over. I had to climb out of my emotional hell and force Fr. Martin to end his destruction of my life. It was time for people to publicly hear the truth and know that Fr. William Martin was a cowardly, vicious liar.

CHAPTER NINE

# And Ye Shall Know the Truth


The conclusion that Fr. Martin had to be stopped was easy. The hard part was how to do it. If Bishop Shimpfky had refused to utter one simple sentence that could have ended Martin's lies, and no St. John's Church official or parishioner had the curiosity or courage to question even one of the statements he'd repeatedly made, who would stop him? If I were to ask a male friend of mine to tell him to stop slandering me, Fr. Martin would probably hysterically scream that he'd been assaulted.

He'd already done that when Carole went to his office to ask why he'd refused me Communion on Ash Wednesday.[13] At first, he denied it. And, when she said that there were witnesses and that he was unfit to "wear the cloth," he again denied it, hollering loudly, three times, for his secretary to come in. When the secretary rushed in, he instructed her, "Get her out of here. Call the police." Carole told Fr. Martin that would not be the end of it and walked out. Fr. Martin twisted that encounter into a false claim that she had threatened him with an umbrella. She had no umbrella with her when she went to the church around 1:30 PM. Weather records for that date show that there was a light rain beginning at approximately 4:00 PM.

William Martin had—and most likely still has—a remarkable ability to contort almost anything to protect himself and to transfer blame to others. A well-meaning acquaintance of mine remarked that if she were in my place, she would sell her house and leave town. That was one solution, and maybe it would have been the best one for her, but there was no way that I would

13    Coincidentally, Fr. Martin's birthday

surrender to coerced guilt like Franz K. in *The Trial*[14]. If there were going to be anyone on trial, it would have to be Fr. Martin. And that was the decision I made.

Clifford, in his still lingering, soft, Georgia accent opined, "You do what you have to do. A man can be tarnished and thrown to the lions, but people accept it and they overlook it, and he is just a good old Joe. You do a lady this way and it is a scar for life. We're in a small town—*clear your name.*"

The big risk, of course, was that I could lose, and it was more likely than not that I would. Having been in the legal business for eleven years, I knew as well as anyone that lawsuits were to be avoided. The other drawbacks were that it could harm St. John's, which I did not want to do—I still loved my church—even after they had excommunicated and expelled me. And, it could spread Martin's lies even further.

But, they had gone so far already and had made my life such a humiliation, that I had little left to lose. It had to be done. Not only that, but if I didn't stop him, who would? Before long, it would be too late because so many in the church's hierarchy, like Bishop Shimpfky, had covered up for him already that they would have to keep doing it or expose themselves for the deceitful hypocrites they were. I'm no heroine and had no wish to be one, but rational intelligence told me that he would not change. He'd do it again to someone else, probably a woman, because he'd never dare to do it to a man.

I couldn't find an attorney in Monterey to take my case, and a friend referred me to Gordon, who finally agreed to represent me after keeping me dangling for weeks with his indecision. By the time he'd agreed to take my case, he was familiar with the situation. He charged $300 an hour and wanted a $3,000 retainer, which by then seemed to be doing me a favor, albeit a $3,000 favor. In our first official consultation, Gordon asked me what I wanted. Because I wasn't after money, I was unsure how to

14    A novel by Franz Kafka

respond so I answered, "I want an apology." When Gordon heard that, he said, "Maybe we can settle this." He promptly called Andy Swartz, Fr. Martin's attorney, ran through the situation with him, and suggested a settlement. Mr. Swartz grabbed the chance. I was so relieved at the prospect of not having to proceed with a full-blown lawsuit that I didn't wonder how we so instantly arrived at a settlement. When I had the chance to think more about it, I wondered if Gordon and Swartz had already discussed the situation. After all, they were "good friends," according to Gordon.

Gordon wrote out the statements that I wanted Fr. Martin to admit were lies, called Swartz back, read them to him, and suggested that Swartz draft the agreement. He added my request that Fr. Martin would pay half of my $3,000 attorney fee, and it was agreed. After Gordon hung up the phone, I said, "Wait a minute. He should pay the whole thing. This isn't *my* fault." Gordon refused to call Swartz back because, "Andy's a good friend of mine, and I'm not going to call him again."

I knew that attorneys regularly saw each other in court, met at social events, belonged to the same clubs, and were sometimes good friends, but when it came to representation of a client, the interests of the client were supposed to take precedence. It was only a phone call and a reasonable request, but I had the feeling that if I argued with Gordon, he might tell me to go elsewhere and there was no elsewhere. It was Gordon or no one, and he'd secured what I had most wanted and asked for—an apology.

The four page agreement, already signed by Swartz and Fr. Martin, along with a check for $1500 was hand-delivered the next day. The admissions I'd sought were spelled out correctly on the first page, but there was no apology. Because Swartz had left out the apology—I believed intentionally—I refused to sign. Gordon was very upset with my refusal and tried to convince me that the agreement had everything. It did not. The only thing I'd asked for all along—an apology—was not there. He called my attention to the check, lying between us on his desk, as though money had been my motive or would persuade me. It felt like an added insult, and I still refused to sign. Gordon had to call his "good friend" and tell him that I wouldn't sign. Swartz was angry, too. They acted as though the apology was no big deal, and I was being an unreasonable, demanding woman.

Swartz finally agreed to insert an apology, but threatened that if I refused to sign again, the deal was off. Because his initial response had been so fast, I believed he wanted the agreement as much as I did. As an attorney, he had to know the situation his client was in and the importance of getting him out of it as quickly as possible. I'm quite sure that he would have agreed to the full $3,000 if Gordon had called him back as I'd asked him to.

Once again, the amended document was promptly returned by hand delivery. The apology consisted of only four words, "for which I apologize." It wasn't much, but to me it was a very big deal.

Gordon signed on the last page and slid the agreement across his desk for me to sign, which I did. When he handed me the $1500 check, he said, "Now you can go back to your church." He seemed genuinely pleased, and I certainly was.

The following first page of the settlement agreement has the admissions and apology, pages two and three are standard legal boilerplate, and the last page is the signature page.

### "MUTUAL RELEASE

This Settlement Agreement and Mutual General Release has been entered into by and between William Martin (hereinafter "Martin") and Rayn Random (hereinafter "Random).

**Recitals**

a. Martin is now and has been the minister of St. John's Chapel for several years and Random has from time to time attended functions at that Chapel.

b. In or about 2004 and 2005[15], Random claims that Martin

---

15      The correct years are 2002, 2003, 2004, 2005

made certain disparaging remarks about Random to third parties generally and certain members of the St. John's Chapel specifically.

c. The parties now desire to resolve any and all matters between them and in consideration of the promise and representations herein, mutually agree as follows:

**Operative Provision**

1. Martin issues the following statement: "I made the following untrue statements about Ms. Random for which I apologize: (a) She tried to lure me into her hot tub; (b) It was necessary for me to get a restraining order against her. No restraining order was necessary nor obtained; (c) That she was a man and not a woman; (d) her breasts were false; (e) she made inappropriate advances towards me; (f) she had stalked me; (g) she had made numerous harassing telephone calls which required me to change my telephone number.

"I admit that Ms. Random warned me to stop making such false representations concerning whether there had been anything about our relationship that involved romantic overtures."

Because Swartz drafted the agreement, he was able to word it favorably to Fr. Martin wherever he could. For example, by saying that I "from time to time attended functions" at St. John's, he set the precedent for future attempts to make me appear as only an occasional visitor. In actuality, I'd attended almost every Sunday from June, 2000 until I was excommunicated in March, 2004. I'd probably been there more Sundays than Fr. Martin, as he always took a month of vacation each year and increasingly more holidays and "retreats" that required substitute priests. Some Sundays, there was no priest at all because Fr. Martin claimed that he had food poisoning and would phone in sick early on Sunday mornings.

Fr. Martin and Swartz wanted the agreement kept confidential. That was unbelievably ridiculous. How would I get my reputation back if it were kept a secret? Why had we bothered to even create the agreement? I assured them that I would not publish it in the Monterey *Herald*, but I would certainly not keep it secret. Everyone who had heard the lies had to learn the truth. We agreed that I would send it to "those persons who she knows, or has reasonable cause to believe, have been recipients of such false information."

The first page was the most important, and that was all I intended to send. But, having grown a little wiser, I realized it would invite criticism and suspicion that there was something to hide in the other pages, so I sent all four of the pages. Only one recipient claimed to not have heard any of Fr. Martin's statements, and I think she just didn't want to admit that she had listened to them. After the letters were mailed, some who received them suggested that other people, whom I had never even heard of —as far away as Salinas and Carmel Valley—should also be sent a copy of the admissions, because they had also heard Fr. Martin's claims.

Clifford insisted that I send one to Joan Fontaine, the actress who'd won an Academy Award for her performance in Alfred Hitchcock's film, *Suspicion*. I had never seen her except in her many movies. I knew the St. John's rose garden was originally donated by her, and she had once been married there, but I didn't know that she and Fr. Martin were friends and that he had been a guest in her home many times when he made me a topic of conversation.

According to Clifford, Fr. Martin told Ms. Fontaine that he had to get a restraining order against me, "She's stalking me, she's in love with me, or she's got the 'hots' for me…always trying to get me in her hot tub. She has pictures of me throughout her home, that's how obsessed she is." Clifford told Ms. Fontaine those things weren't true, but she didn't believe him at the time. He insisted, "Joan, some way, somehow I'm going to prove to you this is incorrect."

After Ms. Fontaine received a copy of the agreement, she told him, "Cliff, I can hardly believe my eyes. This is just, I don't know, repulsive, terrible. How could someone in his position—in a clergy's position—do this?"

As to the photos all over my house, Clifford said in his deposition, "I was in (Rayn Random's) kitchen, no photo. I was in her living room, no photo. I was in her bedroom, no photo. I was in her dressing room because it looks out over the pine trees we discussed earlier, no photo. And I was in her guest bathroom, and there was no photo." Walter later testified to the same thing— there were no photos.

The truth was out at last. I thought that everything necessary to restore my name and reputation had been accomplished. I was thrilled that I could return to my church and was anxious to do so. Bob, now attending St. Mary's in protest against Fr. Martin, was overjoyed at the admission and apology. He wanted to return with me, and we agreed to meet just before the 10:30 service on the second Sunday after signing of the agreement. I looked forward to seeing Bob and the few people I believed were still my friends.

On that Sunday, it was cold and misty, a typical March morning in Monterey. I found a parking space from which I could watch the church steps for Bob and backed into it to wait. I didn't want to attract attention and was glad that people kept their heads down while they hurried into church to escape the weather. My car wasn't recognized because I was driving a rental while mine was being repaired, and no one seemed to recognize or even notice me. At least, I didn't think so.

The choir arrived at the church steps, followed by Fr. Martin, and they all went inside. There were three people still standing together at the foot of the steps, hunched over and moving around in an apparent effort to keep warm. I thought it strange that they remained outside in the cold and wet. When I turned on the ignition key to see the time and it was 10:35, I realized that Bob must already be inside, so I hurried toward the church.

When I got to the foot of the steps, the three people

immediately stepped in front of me, shoulder to shoulder, and physically blocked me. When I attempted to walk around them, they stepped sideways in unison to stop me again. I recognized Howard Sitton on the right, but the two women were nondescript in baggy black clothes, and I had no idea who they were. Finally, the one in the middle said she was Pamela Norton, the Senior Warden, and she demanded that I leave

I intended to stand my ground. I wasn't going to let this go unchallenged as I had with Howard Sitton a year earlier. I confidently asked her, "Have you read the document that Fr. Martin signed?"

She answered contemptuously that she didn't need to read it because she already knew it. In a bragging, sneering way she said, "We knew all about it even before it was signed. We met in Andy Swartz's office, and then he came and talked to us (the vestry) at church. He told us that Fr. Martin only signed it to get rid of you so we could move on. The whole church took a vote, and we are supporting Fr. Martin."

It was such an unexpected encounter, and I was so stunned by her claim, that it took a moment to process what she was saying. When I—once again—didn't leave immediately, Howard Sitton said, "Rayn, you're not wanted here..." They were acting like street thugs protecting their turf from a hated rival gang member, and not at all like the Christians that they seemed to think they were. It was futile to try to pass all three of them, or to say anything more. I looked at each of their smug faces glaring at me and said, "You're all hypocrites," and left.

Bob called me when he got home, wondering why I hadn't shown up. I told him what had happened, and he related that he had seen Fr. Martin after the service and said to him, "I was supposed to meet Rayn here this morning. I wonder why she didn't come." Fr. Martin never said a word.

I had believed the same as Gordon, it was over, and I could go back to my church. But, obviously, we were both wrong. In the brief time between signing the agreement and that Sunday, while I had been happily anticipating my return to St. John's, Fr. Martin and his personal disciples—the vestry—had also been anticipating my return, but not with the same joyfulness, and they were several steps ahead of me, literally as well as figuratively.

Just as Pamela Norton had said, she, as Senior Warden, and probably Sitton knew about the agreement ahead of time, but all they knew was that I, "the troublemaker,"[16] was threatening Fr. Martin and the purpose of the agreement was to finally "get rid of" me once and for all. At a meeting only five days after the signing of the agreement, Andy Swartz met with the vestry at the church—just as Ms. Norton had said—and assured them that Fr. Martin had signed the admission only to get rid of me. Fr. Martin then recanted to the vestry, claimed that what he'd said about me was true, and he'd signed the agreement only to avoid litigation and publicity.

Anita Steel gave an account of the meeting. She related under oath, "Andy Swartz came to the vestry meeting, and Fr. Martin essentially told the vestry that he was doing this to get rid of her—to just make this go away, and we can all keep going down the road and be happy. The problem was, I spoke to Pam Norton, and she said she was with, and a part of, the discussion of this agreement and settlement that had been created. The truth is, I had never seen this document, nor had anyone else on the vestry ever seen this document we were talking about, nor the wording, nor the accusations that Fr. Martin was…agreeing to have made. We had heard those accusations, he had made them to us, but we had never seen it on paper. Never, until I got Rayn Random's letter, did any of us ever see this." Ms. Steel said the only discussion of the agreement was the one held *after* it was signed and mailed.

---

16    The vestry passed a resolution that I was never to be referred to by name. I was always a "former attendee" or the "troublemaker." It also resolved that Fr. Martin was never to be subjected to any review.

She continued to describe the meeting and recalled, "Bettina McBee is the only other person...besides myself, who ever stood up in shock when we were presented this. Bettina brought her Bible and her small child with her to this vestry meeting and was in tears and crying, and desperately saying to him (Fr. Martin), 'This document you signed says this is true, that you say you did all this and they are untrue (now) when you tell us you did this just to get rid of her. Yet you signed that. You paid her money.'

"It became a very destructive meeting for this vestry. Fr. Martin, instead of accepting it and discussing it with her—as I'm trying to hold her hand and hold her crying child—screamed and yelled at her and told her that she didn't know what she was talking about, that there was one thing that needed to be done, and the only thing that needed to be done was to *get rid of Rayn Random*, and that's what this was about. If she didn't like it, she should leave—and she left."

The official minutes of that meeting were tidied up and condensed to just one sentence as follows:

"Rector's Report: Fr. Martin commented on the recent unpleasantness with a former attendee, and that the mutual release and settlement agreement which had been entered into to avoid litigation and publicity had been made very public since she has sent it to many congregation members."

The "Rector's Report" is a perfect example of how Fr. Martin can write something—completely factual—but totally misleading.

Not only were people assigned to watch for me on Sundays, they had even created what they called *The Red Book* and kept it handy so that someone could quickly phone the police if I appeared. It had a pre-written statement that they were supposed to read to the police.

The statement was, "There is an individual on our property who was told by the Standing Committee of the Episcopal Diocese of El Camino Real...and by the Vestry of St. John's...and by our former Bishop, Richard Shimpfky, that she was not, and is not, to return to St. John's Chapel. She is trespassing on private property and we require a police officer to escort her off of the property. Could we please have some assistance?"

After I'd returned home following my Sunday morning encounter with Sitton and friends, I was quite confident that Gordon could straighten everything out. Because it was Fr. Martin's lies that had caused my excommunication, and since he had confessed—in writing—that they were lies, surely it would be my right to return. On Monday, I phoned Gordon and left a message asking him to call me. That call and several others went unanswered, as did a letter to which he never replied. By my calculation he'd spent no more than five hours, at the very most, on my case. I had a lot more time left on his books and deserved a response from him. I assume that he didn't respond because he didn't want to call his "good friend" Andy Swartz on my behalf. Neither, did he return any portion of the $3,000 retainer.

So, that was it. No church, no attorney, no recourse. I was moving from disappointment in what claimed to be a church of God, to anger and disgust directed mostly at myself. I was right back where I'd been before the agreement was signed. But now, it was even worse because in return for Fr. Martin signing the agreement, I'd given up my right to sue him. It had never entered my mind that he would take back his admission. I'd trusted the same lying, deceitful priest, *again!* I had signed the agreement in good faith, and I had made a huge mistake. I'd even added to it because now, I was the despicable woman who had falsely accused "such a fine priest," as Bishop Shimpfky referred to him, and I was the one accused of lying, not Fr. Martin.

The only person in the Episcopal Church hierarchy, other than retired Fr. Wolter, who cared about what had transpired was Fr. Hansen in Carmel. I phoned him and we met in his office. He told me that it would be of no use to even try to speak to the St. John's vestry because they probably wouldn't agree to a meeting, and if they did, they wouldn't believe anything I said.

He suggested that I appeal to the Diocese Standing Committee, the same committee that had brought charges against Bishop Shimpfky. In the absence of a permanent bishop, they now shared authority with the recently-appointed interim Bishop Romero. Fr. Hansen phoned the committee president, Ann Wright, and told her that I needed to speak with her.

Before my meeting with her at the diocese offices, I prepared a written summary of everything that had taken place, including a copy of the settlement agreement. When she opened the door to an office for us, there was Bishop Romero waiting to participate in our meeting. I hadn't expected that, and when I held out my hand as she introduced us, he pulled me to him—against him— and hugged me. It felt awful, and I was offended by his extremely inappropriate behavior. That was not the moment, however, for me to express my opinion. I mentally tried to excuse it as a cultural difference, but I'd lived in Central America and I knew it was not appropriate.

We sat around a rectangular coffee table that had a couch on one side and a large upholstered chair at each end. Ms. Wright sat on the couch, and Bishop Romero and I faced each other across the table. Since I hadn't expected the Bishop to join us, I had only one extra copy of everything and I gave it to Ms. Wright. As I went through all of the events in more detail, it appeared to me that Ms. Wright was quite shaken. Bishop Romero, however, sat emotionless and motionless. Each time I looked at him, I couldn't help thinking that he looked like a fat toad dressed in priestly clothes, basking in garden sunshine. His corpulence had settled itself deep into the chair, and he didn't move except to blink his eyes periodically, his expression remaining completely unresponsive to the information I was conveying. Not a flinch, or even a look of disbelief, crossed his placid face. I concluded my narrative with a request for a full and impartial investigation as required by Episcopal Church Canon Law—which appears on the ECUSA official web site.

Bishop Romero spoke at last and asked, "Why do you think Fr. Martin did those things?"

I said, "I don't know."

Then he gave me a knowing, condescending look that I had learned to recognize and said, "Well, you must have done *something*." I sensed right then that his mind had already been made up even before I'd arrived and that my presentation had been an effort in futility. I was offended by his statement and let it show in my voice

I looked him straight in the eye and could feel my jaw tighten as I said slowly and firmly, "I've done nothing."

His reply was stunning. He said, with the presumptuous superiority of one who believes that only *he* knows the truth, "Perhaps it's a question of lifestyle." It clearly wasn't Fr. Martin's lifestyle he was referring to—it was *mine*. I had no answer for his insult. As though all of this had been news to him, he said that he would speak with Fr. Martin about the matter. As I got up to leave, he also stood, extended his hand and then *pulled me against him again* while he mumbled some kind of blessing. It was gross, and my mind screamed, "How *dare* you!" I was furious with myself for not seeing it coming, and it was even more offensive after what he had said to me. It was disrespectful, inappropriate, and I felt as though I had been violated. But this was my last chance, and I chose not to destroy it with an ill-considered response. Ann Wright walked to the door with me, and when I looked at her face as I was leaving, I believed she was near to tears.

Later when I told a friend that the Bishop was going to speak to Fr. Martin, he just smiled at me and said, "Rayn, he talked to Fr. Martin before you ever got there." My friend was even more correct than he'd thought because, just as Fr. Martin had set me up with his email to Bishop Shimpfky before I met with him in 2003, Fr. Martin's devoted attorney, Andrew Swartz—Gordon's "good friend"—wrote a letter that set me up for the Standing Committee's investigation and my meeting with Ann Wright and

Bishop Romero. I say he wrote it just for that occasion because there was no logical explanation for Swartz to write the letter *two months after Martin had already signed the admission.* Mr. Swartz *created* an exciting scenario and reasons for the admission that were guaranteed to convince anyone—including a bishop—that I should be hauled off to the loony bin as a matter of public safety.

Mr. Swartz wrote the letter on his law firm's "Spiering, Swartz & Kennedy, Attorney's at Law" letterhead[17] and addressed it to Rev. William Martin. Mr. Swartz wrote:

"It is appropriate to summarize why I recommended that you sign the settlement agreement with Rayn Random. First, and foremost, it is my opinion that she is somewhat psychotic and desperate and that it is important to defuse the situation before she further interferes with you and St. John's Chapel. Second, it is prudent, especially in today's society, to avoid litigation with such a person who is only looking for a stage on which to perpetuate her confused and misguided perception of the world. Third, it avoids any potential publicity. Fourth, the cost is minimal. You paid her nothing. We simply agreed to reimburse her lawyer a small portion of the legal fees he charged to Random. Fifth, we included a statement in the release, and Random agreed and acknowledged as follows:

"This agreement shall in no way be construed as an admission by any party that any of them have acted wrongfully or that any of them have any rights or claims against the other.

"Sixth: I know you expressed your feelings concerning faith and forgiveness that are very important to you. For all of the above, you decided to settle with Random with which decision I strongly agree.

"Finally, given the dangerous and unpredictable nature of this lady, I strongly recommend that she never be allowed back

---

17      I wonder how Swartz's law partners, Mr. Spiering and Ms. Kennedy, feel about his using their company letterhead to libel someone. That letter is not protected, unlike the lies he later told in a courtroom.

into St. John's Chapel or near you or your flock. She is manipulative and has already violated the confidentiality provision of the settlement agreement in numerous ways.[18] She cannot be trusted to act appropriately. If you need any additional information, please do not hesitate to contact me. Thank you for allowing me to be of service to you. Sincerely, Andrew H. Swartz"

The letter was marked "Confidential Attorney Client." However, when Fr. Martin presented the letter to Bishop Romero, he broke the attorney/client confidentiality.

I was furious and actually physically sickened when I saw a copy of that letter two years later. How could Andrew Swartz, a man who had *never met me* nor spoken one word to me, make up such a vicious document for the sole purpose of destroying me, a woman whom he apparently decided should be quickly disposed of by any expedient method short of murder? And what kind of motive inspired him to devise his hate-filled attack in defense of a man, whom he should have realized by that time, was a despicable liar despite the priest's collar he wore.

---

18      Another lie from Mr. Swartz—there was no confidentially clause in the agreement that he, himself, drafted.

# CHAPTER TEN

# Thus It Is Written

The Standing Committee's investigation took more than six weeks, leading me to believe that they were being extraordinarily thorough in seeking the truth, although it was strange that no one from the committee contacted me for an interview. Several times I was tempted to inquire whether they wanted to question me, but I convinced myself that they knew what they were doing and were taking their investigation seriously. In late May their report finally arrived. It consisted of a brief, one-page letter written on Diocese of El Camino Real letterhead. It read:

"Dear Ms. Random:

"As you requested in your letter of April 4, 2005, and your meeting with Bishop Romero and Ann Wright, the Ecclesiastical Authority has investigated the matter and concluded that Fr. William Martin acted within his discretion under the Rubics in denying you Communion at St. John's Chapel. The investigation has concluded that your presence and behavior at St. John's Chapel have been disruptive and distressful to the congregation and to individual members as has been conveyed to you by the wardens and vestry on more than one occasion.

"With the Spirit's guidance, we hope you will return to Holy Communion at another parish or mission."

It was signed: The Rev. Christopher Creed, Vice-president of the Standing Committee/Ecclesiastical Authority. And, being a devoted disciple of our Lord, he also drew a small cross after his name.

My reaction was disbelief. I knew it had been a sham investigation, even though I had no idea at the time that they had called no witnesses, and that the investigation consisted solely of a conversation with Fr. Martin and a phone call to Pamela Norton that she could not even remember receiving. I had been treated with disrespect and contempt, instead of fairness and impartiality.

A year later, we discovered an email that Ann Wright wrote to Creed —one day after his letter to me—May 24, 2005.

"Hi! Hope Clergy Conference went well for you.

"The Bishop (Romero) was concerned that we had to send a letter to Rayn telling her that she could not have communion at that church. He knew it would come to this. He just doesn't like to see people turned away for reasons such as Bill (Fr. Martin) explained. I think part of his discomfort is that Bill Martin has nothing to do with the diocese and yet comes to us when in trouble. He feels Bill wants to do his own thing and not be accountable. I think he sees that both parties are at fault and this was *an easy way* to *get rid of a problem*. He had never said this before and, of course, *we did what we had to do*. Just thought I would let you know. He said it was a good thing a lawyer wrote the letter. It would have been hard for him to do."

By November 28, 2006, when we took Ann Wright's deposition, she seemed to have undergone a metamorphosis, or perhaps a trauma, that affected her ability to recall certain events. In particular, that I had related Martin's behavior and lies to both her and Bishop Romero, I had given her a letter containing the same information, and that she had a copy of Martin's signed admissions. A month prior to our meeting, Bishop Romero also had a copy of the admissions that I had intended for Bishop Shimpfky. However, the diocese secretary, whose attitude toward me was the same as all the others in the diocese—contempt, with not the slightest effort to conceal it—had refused to give me Shimpfky's new address, but offered to send the copy for me. But, after I'd given the copy to her, she declared that she was going to give it to Bishop Romero, instead. I protested that I wanted Shimpfky to see the truth and that Romero didn't know what it was all about, but she still flat out refused to send it.

Under oath, and after introductory questioning by Neil Shapiro, he asked Ms. Wright, "What is the function of the Standing Committee?" She said that it "serves as a body of advice to the bishop," and when there is not a bishop, but an assisting bishop such as Romero was, "the Standing Committee becomes the ecclesiastical authority by Canon Law." Shapiro inquired, "Have you had any training or instruction in Canon Law?" and she answered, "No." She further stated that she had no idea as to whether the diocese must approve the hiring of a rector by a church within the diocese, nor did she have any knowledge as to whether the diocese had the authority to impose discipline on a rector of a church within the diocese.

When Neil asked Ms. Wright whether she had read the letter I had presented to her at our April, 2005 meeting she said, "I don't remember whether I did or not." Shapiro continued, "If I understand you correctly, previously you said you were not aware that Rayn Random was accusing William Martin of making disparaging or untrue statements about her until the meeting. Do you recall what Ms. Random said…that made you aware of that fact?"

Although my letter, Exhibit 48, stated, "On March 5, 2005, Bill Martin signed the *attached* admission and apology," Ms. Wright said, "I believe that what I remember was some comments that she made concerning membership in her church, in the church, and the fact that she had been denied communion. That's about all I remember at that conversation."

Shapiro asked—including up to the present time—"did you ever become aware that Rayn Random accused William Martin of making false and disparaging statements about her?" She said, "*No.*"

"Did you ever see a document singed by William Martin in which it says, 'Willliam Martin makes the following statement… for which I apologize' and then lists seven of them?"

She answered, *"No,"* and when he confirmed her reply, "You never saw that document?" She said, *"No, I don't recall that at all."* She also claimed to know nothing about the investigation, but she said, "I believe that Father Creed did write a letter to Ms. Random as a result of any investigation that was done."

It was stunning to hear her say that she *believed* Creed wrote me a letter. She knew all about the letter to me, and I do not believe she could have forgotten her own email to Creed, nor can I believe that she couldn't remember what I told her during my visit to the diocese, and the letter and copy of the agreement which she kept.

Finally Shapiro inquired, "Do you have any recollection of anything that was said at the meeting, other than the mention of church membership and denial of Communion?"

Ms. Wright answered, "No."

It was clear to me that Ms. Wright had fit in very well with Christopher Creed, Bishop Romero, and the Episcopal Diocese of El Camino Real.

On the advice which Fr. Creed gave me in his letter—that I act "with the Spirit's guidance"—I did exactly that by letting him know how I felt about the Standing Committee's supposed investigation. My June 7, 2005 letter to Fr. Creed stated in part:

"I remind you that William Martin is a self-confessed liar who has broken the Ninth Commandment,[19] which appears not to have disturbed anyone on your committee. You have in essence conducted a Star Chamber hearing. You have recited no evidence to support your conclusion that my 'presence and behavior at St. John's have been disruptive and distressful to the congregation and to individual members.'

"My presence at St. John's Chapel has distressed only one person and that is William Martin, caused by his own unresolved fantasies and imaginings, not by anything I have done or any behavior on my part."

---

19     Thou shalt not bear false witness against thy neighbor.

In closing, I demanded the names of those who testified and the charges they made against me, saying I had a right to confront my accusers. Needless to say, he never answered the letter.

When Shapiro later asked him why not, he said he never saw it, but that he "must have received it." Of course, there was no list of accusers that he could have provided because there was only one accuser—William Martin. He couldn't very well admit that there were no others. What William Martin told them, along with Attorney Swartz's psychological expertise,[20] had perhaps been sufficient—that I was "psychotic and desperate, had a confused and misguided perception of the world," and that I was "dangerous and unpredictable."

Still inspired by "the Spirit's guidance," I didn't let Bishop Romero escape my anger either. I wrote a letter requesting a meeting with him. I said that I had been puzzled by his statements and asked him to explain what he meant by them. I offered to accommodate his schedule at any time he chose, and I never heard from him either. In his deposition he said, "If this letter had come to me with something like that, I would have answered it because I know I did not say that." Under oath, wearing his clerical collar, and sitting directly across the table from me—even closer than at our diocese meeting—Bishop Romero lied. He piously continued, "I know I would not say something like that." He avoided looking at me throughout his entire questioning, but I hoped he felt the scorch of my angry focus on him.

The Standing Committee had been the last resort available within the church. They'd abandoned their obligation to follow church canon law, and as a result of their laziness, indifference, and arrogance, my reputation was still lying crumpled in the dirt. Thankfully, many of those who had originally believed Fr. Martin had changed their minds after reading his admissions, while others continued to believe him despite reading the agreement,

---

20      A physician friend suggested that I file a complaint with the California State Medical Board that Mr. Swartz was practicing medicine without a license.

and they even felt anger toward me for exposing the truth, a fact that I found incomprehensible.

During a party at the Carmel Women's Club, Walter was in the middle of a conversation with a lady when she interrupted him mid-sentence, pointed to a woman in the room and said, "Is that the woman who's stalking Fr. Martin?" It wasn't me, as I had declined to attend—exactly because of people like her—but she was anxious, even excited, to get a look at "the woman." She adamantly refused to believe Walter when he told her Fr. Martin had admitted in writing that he'd lied. It frustrated both Walter and Clifford that people were having such salacious enjoyment at my expense while refusing to listen to the truth. Later that day, Walter and Clifford took a copy of the agreement to the lady's home, and even after reading for herself, a signed, legal document admitting to his lies, she still refused to believe it. She continued to invite him to her parties, and he continued to accept.

Clifford repeatedly urged me to get back into a social life, but any self confidence I'd managed to hang on to was gone, and I preferred to avoid glares and disgusted looks by staying home. However, he did convince me to attend the Monterey Civic Club's 100th anniversary celebration which he was chairing. The event attracted a large crowd, and the experience was typical. Anyone who didn't know me was friendly, but five women members, including Adrianne, showed me an attitude colder than the ice in the Champagne punch that I was serving.

While I was being treated like a woman with a scarlet letter on her forehead, Fr. Martin remained a favored guest at parties. Many Monterey hostesses considered it a social coup to have a priest at their parties, especially an unmarried, intelligent, good looking one, who drank and smoked and was charismatically entertaining. He thoroughly enjoyed regaling people with his stories of the crazed woman who was stalking him, had tried to lure him into her hot tub, had called him with lurid proposals, and was obsessed with him. This was mighty juicy gossip for party guests all over the Peninsula where police calls reported in the *Carmel Pine Cone*, for example, are rarely more exciting than an elderly woman being unable to find her keys after having cocktails with friends at La Cuesta on a Friday evening.

Fr. Martin's stories could and did liven up any occasion. Everyone who heard his lies passed them on to others, spreading them like a newly mutated, virulent virus. The more he said, the more people could ask him at their next meeting, "Is 'that woman' still stalking you?" He could show them a pained and brave face like the one he displayed for Carole in the market, roll his eyes, slowly shake his head, and lament how much it distressed him. It was "poor Fr. Martin," all over again.

While my detractors were verbally feasting on the carcass of my reputation, I was losing at every attempt to resuscitate it. I drifted further into a state of depression. I didn't sleep well and had frightening dreams. The one that recurred most often was that I was trapped all alone on narrow streets in a blackened city at night, surrounded by tall, massive, dark buildings with no lighted windows. Only the intersections had light and that was one bare light bulb. Everywhere I turned led to more of the same and I would be seized by panic because I couldn't find my way out. Occasionally I came across people in small groups, but they were as scary as the streets, and I was afraid to approach them. No dream analysis was required to figure those dreams out. I lost interest in almost everything and had to drag myself to accomplish even minimum tasks. One friend urged me to see a psychiatrist and gave me a name, "just to talk about it." I didn't need to examine every childhood disappointment or hurt feeling. The cause was obvious, and it was a "who," not a "what." A psychiatrist would prescribe medication to make me feel better about my own living demise, and there was no way I would step into that vortex.

In late August 2005, Bob, who had returned to St. Mary's Episcopal Church in protest, again, of William Martin, phoned me. He said that a deacon there was a friend of his, and he had told the deacon about me. Bob gave me a phone number and said the man, Les Reed, was expecting my call.

Les and I met for lunch at his favorite restaurant where everyone knew him, and it didn't take long to discover why he had an uncountable number of friends who treasured him. His beautiful eyes reflected an equally beautiful soul that exuded warmth, kindness, and an absolute love of God and all of His creations. He seemed almost ageless, though I would surmise he was in his late sixties. He always wore a cross, and it was refreshing to see someone wearing that symbol *who actually believed in it,* rather than the cynical use the Episcopal priests and bishops put it to by drawing it after their signatures.

Les listened to my story without comment and when I'd finished he said, very slowly and with great sadness, "I can't believe it." He shook his head and paused a moment before reassuring me, "I believe you…*but I can't believe it.* I've been in the Episcopal Church a long, long time. I've heard everything, and I've seen everything, but I have *never* heard anything like this." He was silent, and I said nothing so as to not disturb his thoughts when he suddenly declared, "You've got to go back! You *have* to go back. This has got to be cleansed. It can't be covered over any longer."

The thought of going back was something I didn't want to even contemplate, much less actually do. I saw nothing to be gained by deliberately inviting insults from people I regarded as unthinking, misguided zealots acting out an imagined mission from God, as revealed to them by their "spiritual leader." But when Les said he would go with me, that changed everything— including my mind—and we set a date. Sadly, when the time came, Les was in the hospital. When I went to see him he insisted that I had to go without him. I wouldn't go alone, but in the interim I'd become accepting of the idea of challenging William Martin and his sycophants who were turning my beloved St. John's Chapel into a cult. I mentioned to Les that Walter and Clifford had been urging my return and he immediately commanded, "Go with them!" It was too risky to argue with a man who'd just had a heart attack, and his forcefulness had rekindled the spark of determination that was still left in me. I promised I would go.

Walter and Clifford were overjoyed at my decision because they didn't want Fr. Martin to think he'd escaped all consequences for what he had done to me and that it had all been forgotten. We went the next Sunday—October 16, 2005. We arrived a few minutes early, before the choir had gathered at the foot of the steps. No one recognized our SUV, and there didn't seem to be anyone standing guard. Howard Sitton was at the door handing out the programs, and I was the first one to reach the door. He gave me a program and when he realized who I was, it was too late to stop me. He didn't know who Walter and Clifford were, or that they were with me, until we sat together with Bob, who had wanted to lend his support and was already waiting in our pew. I sat next to Bob, then Walter, and then Clifford on the aisle. I read in the program that there was a visiting priest from Uganda that day and, as was the custom, he would deliver the sermon and assist Fr. Martin in serving Holy Communion. We all agreed not to take Communion from Fr. Martin.

The congregation stood to sing the opening hymn and the choir—led by David Jones (the man I had encountered at Orchard Supply) carrying the processional cross—made its way to the front of the church, the two priests walking side by side behind it. When they passed our pew Fr. Martin must have seen *us* because that was the last we saw of *him*. Knowing how cowardly he is, my guess is that he told his visitor from Uganda to continue without him, and he made a panicked departure through the sacristy door by the altar. He certainly didn't want *me* in church and Walter and Clifford were not good news either, as they knew him even better than I did.

With Fr. Martin gone, Bob and I went forward to take Communion. While we were waiting in the aisle to approach the altar, I felt a tap on my shoulder. I braced myself in anticipation that it was Howard Sitton about to tell me to leave, but when I turned around I saw that it was Walter, who had decided to join us. The priest, not knowing who I was or what was happening, gave me a Communion wafer, but when David Jones who was following with the wine got to me, he turned his back and refused me the wine.

Bob saw what happened and was furious. When David came back down the aisle at the end of the service, Bob said, "Hypocrite," loud enough for David to hear it. That was an extraordinary outburst of temper for mild-mannered Bob, who later asked David why he didn't give me the wine. David answered, "It wasn't my choice."

Walter and I decided to attend coffee hour so I could say hello to an English lady that I was very fond of. When we got to Parish Hall, David Jones and Howard Sitton were standing at the open double doors, one on each side. As I attempted to enter, they each slammed a door shut in my face, and Walter's.

Fr. Martin's vanishing act was later explained in the vestry minutes as: "Rector's Report, Remarks: Fr. Martin announced that, as planned, Fr. Jim Short from Uganda was the guest preacher at last Sunday's service, *giving Fr. Martin the opportunity to teach the Sunday school children.*" In my years at St. John's, I don't recall that Fr. Martin ever once taught Sunday school, and he generally showed no interest in children. *If* there were any children present, and often there were none, Sunday school always ended before the church service, and the children then joined their parents in the main church for the last part of the service. I saw no children come into the church that Sunday. Also, Fr. Martin would normally have joined Fr. Short to greet parishioners as they exited the church. He did not. Father Short stood alone.

In his written account of that day's events, Sitton wrote, "Father Martin, who had been informed of the presence of Rayn Random, left as per his previously arranged schedule to teach the Sunday school." Asked by attorney Shapiro, "Did you mean to convey that it was always the intention of William Martin to teach Sunday school that day," Sitton, answered, "Yes."

In his deposition testimony, Howard tried to insist that Fr. Martin's departure had been pre-arranged and that he personally knew it had been so, but when Shapiro asked him how he knew, Sitton said, "That's what I hear." When Shapiro asked if it was customary for Fr. Martin to leave during a visiting priest's sermon to go off and teach Sunday school, Sitton answered, "I don't recall him going off to teach Sunday school, but I don't recall everything."

Shapiro followed up with, "This is the only time you can think of, isn't it, that Fr. Martin left a visiting priest to go teach Sunday school?"

Sitton said, "That's correct. That's the only time I can think of."

Turning to the door closing, Shapiro said, "You then indicate in paragraph 5 that Fr. Martin told you 'he did not want Rayn Random to come into the parish hall following the service.' Is that correct?" Sitton's reply was, "Yes."

After our Sunday visit, it was no surprise that Andy Swartz promptly fired off a letter to me as fast as the Monterey Post Office could deliver it. He wrote, "Common sense tells us that it is best for you to stay away from St. John's Chapel and take Holy Communion elsewhere." And, making certain to cover for his very special client, he added, "Please understand that Fr. Martin was not present when this event occurred..." I already "understood" that very well, indeed, and laughed out loud when I read it. He wasn't present because he ran away. Swartz continued, "And like you, desires only to get on with his life and hopes that you can get on with your life. I certainly hope and trust that a restraining order will not be necessary and that you will attend church elsewhere in the future. Thank you for your anticipated cooperation."

Andy Swartz telling me where I should attend church

and threatening me with, of all things, *a restraining order*, was laughable—and infuriating. I immediately wrote a reply to him in which I said:

"I am pleased to learn that you 'hope and trust that a restraining order will not be necessary.' In the event that your client could manage to obtain a temporary restraining order, the hearing to make it permanent would be extremely interesting. I imagine the court would be quite fascinated to hear the sworn testimony of a man, a priest no less, who has admitted in writing that he previously lied about having a restraining order, as well as other 'untrue statements'[21] about the very person against whom he seeks one." I closed with, "Do not thank me for my 'anticipated cooperation.' You do not have it."

It struck me that Mr. Swartz was beginning to think of himself as an official of St. John's. He represented Fr. Martin only. St. John's Chapel had its own attorney, and it was *not* Andrew Swartz.

I went to see Les who was back at home and breathing from an oxygen tank. When I reported what had happened, he said. "You have to go back next Sunday," and he repeated what he'd said earlier, "You can't wait. This has got to be cleansed." I didn't stay long as he was very weak and it was a struggle for him to speak without a seizure of coughing. That was the last time I saw Les Reed. He died only days later. I knew immediately that his sudden, last minute appearance in my life, just before his death, had happened for a reason. I believed that reason was to set me on the course he had urged: "This must be cleansed to the very bottom," and he had assigned the task to me.

I found out at Les' memorial service that he was not really a deacon although many people thought he was. He was so beloved by everyone that it didn't matter to them, and it didn't matter to me either. In recognition of his service and devotion to the church, clergy and church staff fondly referred to him as the

21    A quote from the agreement that Swartz wrote and Martin signed

"Monsignor"[22]

If it hadn't been for Les' last words to me, I might have given up returning to St. John's, but I decided to go one more time. Besides, I confess—I wanted William Martin to know that he hadn't "won" by running away, or having his attorney threaten me. I wanted him to know that I was there watching him chastise everyone for their sins, while hiding his own transgressions behind his clerical collar—and I knew the truth.

---

22     "Monsignor" is a title of honor in the Roman Catholic Church. The title was "borrowed" to honor Les.

# CHAPTER ELEVEN

# Fear Not

On the following Sunday, Walter, Clifford and I returned to St. John's Chapel and parked at the side of the church, not knowing what might be awaiting us. A serpent must have been waiting for Walter because as we passed by a tree loaded with ripe apples, he wanted to stop and pick a few. As serious as we were that morning, Clifford and I had to laugh as we admonished Walter to remember the Garden of Eden and not "partake of the forbidden fruit."

When we got to the church steps, we recognized the reception committee that awaited our arrival. It was Howard Sitton, a man named Kevin Hulsey who, during a previous marriage, had been a neighbor of Walter and Clifford's, and his present wife Stephanie, who is an assistant district attorney. I was very surprised to see her standing next to the door at the top of the church steps, and it made me wonder if she was there on official business. I had never before seen her at St. John's except when she sang at her father's funeral, but perhaps she attended the early service. And, I had never seen her husband Kevin attend any church functions.

In later trial discovery, I learned that Stephanie's appearance had been purposefully and specifically planned at a St. John's vestry meeting so that if I appeared, Stephanie could stop me from entering. The vestry minutes for that particular meeting indicate that perhaps, even more important to them, she could get the police to St. John's to have me arrested. Vestry minutes do not indicate whether Stephanie was actually at the meeting, or if she participated in the planning, and when we actually arrived at the church, she made no attempt to stop us.

I also learned in our pre-trial discovery that Fr. Martin wanted me to be arrested and urged the vestry members that it had to be done, asking them, "What else can we do?" To rally his loyal troops on Sunday mornings he would say, "She's stalking me. She's stalking me," while seeking people to stand guard when he feared that I might come to church. If I didn't appear, he let it be known how relieved and happy he was. The only thing he had to fear from me was that I could expose him. *It was the truth that he feared—not me.*

As we approached the steps and the sentries took their assigned positions, Kevin Hulsey was the most dramatic of the three, jumping up and down on the steps in front of Clifford, yelling at him that he should leave because, "This isn't your fight!" Howard Sitton assumed his usual position—in my face—and blocking my path. I said, "Good Morning, Howard," and continued up the stairs, always moving to the right so as to go around him, knowing that he didn't dare to touch me because then, I could charge him with assault. Although Kevin and Howard created shouting and turmoil, we all entered the church and Frank Reynolds, who was greeting people at the door and handing out programs, did his little part by indignantly refusing to give us one.

The altar was not set up for Communion that morning, so at least I wouldn't be refused participation. We sat quietly in our same pew, enjoying Clay's preliminary organ selections while waiting for the service to begin. Except for a narrow glimpse down the side aisle, Clay can't clearly see the choir when they gather at the back of the church prior to the service. He starts the first hymn only when he hears Fr. Martin loudly announce it from the rear. The choir had assembled, and Clay played a transition in anticipation of the first hymn announcement. None came.

Clay stretched the transition, then stretched it some more until one of the choir members scurried down the side aisle, trying to not attract attention, to instruct him to keep playing. Everyone noticed. After more minutes, there was still no sign of

Fr. Martin, and people began to look around wondering what was happening. Clay kept playing, and soon a choir member made a second hurried trip to again speak to him. The delay lasted almost twenty minutes, long enough for several of the congregants to turn around and boldly glare at Walter, Clifford, and me, indicating that somehow it had to be our fault. After a while, it became more amusing than uncomfortable, which made it difficult for us to keep straight faces. We knew that something dramatic and frantic had to be happening behind the scenes. It turned out to be far more dramatic and far more frantic than anything we could have imagined.

Finally, Fr. Martin was heard from the rear of the church announcing the first hymn, and the choir proceeded down the center aisle to its place by the altar, followed by Fr. Martin singing loudly as he always did. The service continued with no more delays and no interruptions.

I was informed much later, by two different people, that the reason for the long delay was that Fr. Martin had locked himself in his office and wouldn't come out. One of the choir ladies—I'm told that it was Gaby—had pounded on his door yelling at him without any response until finally, she was driven to *swear* at him and demand that he come out and conduct the service.

During the offering hymn near the end of the service, Frank had another opportunity to act out his hostile feelings. When he passed the collection plate, he refused to offer it to us. Clifford had a check already written and when Frank stopped at the pew behind us, Clifford turned around to put his check in the plate, but Frank quickly snatched it away before Clifford was able to deposit his check.

Following the final blessing, everyone filed out in the usual manner. As I was about to leave our pew, I was stopped by an English couple who always sat behind Bob and me. They were happy to see me and wanted to chat, so I stayed to talk with them, not realizing that soon we were the only ones left in the church.

Clifford called me from the door, and I excused myself.

When I stepped outside at the top of the steps, I had left the sanctuary of God's house and entered a world of the bizarre. As I looked at what lay before me, it resembled the set of an epic Cecil B. DeMill biblical movie: there was the church, St. John's, Christian of course; the heretic, portrayed by me; the righteous hero, smiter of all that is evil, portrayed by Fr. Martin; his loyal and devoted lieutenant, played by Howard Sitton; minor soldiers of the Church, played by themselves; the angry and menacing mob, played by the St. John's congregation; and the Roman Centurions at the ready, prepared to haul me off to the Coliseum and feed me to the lions while the crowd roared along with the lions. The two Centurions were from the Monterey Police Department and had arrived, not in horse drawn chariots, but two super horse-powered police cars.

I was thankful to see the two police officers. Police armed with guns and night sticks were far less fearsome than the St. John's parishioners led by their spiritual advisor, Fr. William Martin.

The police were always polite and they had to follow rules and protocol, unlike anyone associated with St. John's— or the Episcopal Church. Even though I'd never been accosted or questioned by a police officer, when I saw them, I felt a calm settle over me, and the crowd became quickly silent in excited anticipation as I descended the steps toward the officer who was waiting to speak to me. As I approached him, he had a puzzled look on his face. Once again, I wasn't what had been expected. He was probably led to believe that a shrieking, crazy woman would come raging out of the church doors.

He politely introduced himself, and I answered his questions, confirming that I had previously been told to stay away and had been informed that very morning that I was trespassing. I stated that I was not trespassing because, "This is God's house and I have a right to be here." Under the eagerly watchful eyes of the spectators, he made notes of what I said and then used the radio on his shoulder to request a case number assignment. While I watched him and waited, I could hear the crowd of people behind me, but my only concern was that if he took me to jail, someone would have to take care of my dogs and my cat until I got out, which would not be until the next day.

When the reply came over his radio, he wrote the case number on his card and gave it to me. He said that the charge was *Criminal* Trespass, and the case would be turned over to the District Attorney's office to determine whether I should be prosecuted. He said he had the option to arrest me immediately, and I would have to stay in jail until a hearing on Monday, but he chose not to detain me. I was free to go.

So, the Monterey Police Department and the Monterey County Sherriff's Department, in the person of Stephanie Hulsey, were both at St. John's on a Sunday morning because Fr. William J. Martin claimed to be terrified by my presence, and I had dared to attend *his* church. Because of his lies and false witness, I was charged with a criminal offense, actually the second criminal offense he'd charged me with. Stalking had been the first one.

While I was being questioned, in an effort to justify the police having been called, Fr. Martin was anxiously and loudly repeating his claims, especially the stalking one, to the crowd around him. Anita Steel heard him, and at her deposition, Fr. Martin's then attorney, Michael LeVangie, asked her in cross-examination, "Did you mention what you had overheard to anyone else that day?"

Anita paused a moment and looked at him intently as she recalled her feelings. Then, without blinking, she said, "You know what? I mentioned to no one what I'd heard. I, in fact, was in tears."

LeVangie wisely chose not to pursue it and said, "I have no further questions."

When the police departed and I was free to leave, I'm quite certain there was disappointment, especially for William Martin, that I hadn't been handcuffed and thrown into the back of a police car. To my knowledge, Anita Steel was the only person who was saddened by the scene created at St. John's Chapel that Sunday morning. The rest of them were all far beyond the reaches of shame over what they'd just participated in *less than ten minutes after seeking God's forgiveness, singing His praises, and beseeching His blessings—in God's own house!*

Ever the dutiful scribe and lackey, Howard Sitton wrote an account for Fr. Martin in which he said, "The three—a man on either side of RR—proceeded up to the main entrance and I moved into their path. Stephanie and Kevin were there as my witnesses. RR said, 'Good Morning, Howard,' and I said, 'I'm here to tell you, you are trespassing.' RR said, 'No, I'm not.' And I replied, 'Yes, you are.' The heavier man (meaning Clifford) pulled out his cell phone and said, 'Do you want me to call the Sheriff?' I said, 'We will call the police.' Then the man said, 'This is about like Rosa Parks[23]...' I then left to go call the police. Kevin stopped them, trying to reason with them. All I heard as I left was Kevin telling RR, 'You will get in a whole lot of trouble.' I found Dave...talking to the police and reading a copy of the prepared statement...in the front of the *Red Book*."

Howard described what happened when the Monterey Police Department arrived the first time at St. John's. It was just after we had entered the church. "A discussion then ensued regarding the desirability of the officers *going into the church to pick up RR*, and it was decided to ask them to come back toward the end of the service to talk to RR on her way out."

Trying to have me arrested for attending church and filing a complaint against me for a criminal charge based on Martin's false claims dissolved any lingering concerns I had about causing harm to St. John's. I was furious. God no longer existed in that

---

23      Rosa Parks is often called the "mother of the civil rights movement." When she was arrested in 1955 for refusing to give up her seat on a bus to a white man, her courageous action sparked a year long boycott of the bus system. Martin Luther King rose to lead the civil rights movement which culminated in Congress passing the Civil Rights Act of 1964.

church despite the prayer book and the centuries old rituals they observed. By now, most of the congregation had to be aware of what Fr. Martin had been saying for three years, and yet, not one person I was aware of had ever stepped forward on my behalf to ask if what he'd said about me was true. My feeling was, to hell with all of them. And hell is where William Martin was leading them.

Everyone who had even a modicum of authority within the church and could have stopped Martin had covered up and lied for him. Andy Swartz, as far as I could tell, never told Fr. Martin that he'd dodged a bullet when he and I signed our agreement and that he'd better keep his mouth shut in the future, so Fr. Martin felt free to continue his behavior with impunity. It had taken less than two years from our first meeting, if that long, for him to ruin my name in spite of everything I did to try and stop him. With almost thirty years left of his career in the Episcopal Church, I was once again certain that many more reputations and lives would be ruined by him unless *someone* stopped him. The longer that no one dared, the less likely anyone ever would.

It wasn't only Fr. Martin. I was just as sickened by what I'd learned about and experienced from the Episcopal Church hierarchy. The authorities who controlled the church and diocese were also liars and hypocrites who ran the church as though it belonged only to them and its sole purpose was to serve only them, while they merely pretended to serve God. They protected their individual power and did whatever they thought necessary to secure their positions and impress each other. To them, the church was no different than any other corporation, and anyone who didn't go along to get along risked being knocked off the corporate ladder. Or—if the one who refused to go along was a parishioner, he or she could be gotten rid of. Les was right. It had to be cleansed to the very bottom—or perhaps more accurately— to the top.

I had played by the rules, observed all the niceties, assumed that others would live up to their purported integrity, and I had done it patiently and with dignity. In return, the church's leaders and their sycophant followers had demeaned me, damaged my health, destroyed my reputation, and turned me into a sideshow. I would not accept what had been done to me. I couldn't live with myself if I slunk away like the shamed, disgraceful slut that Fr. Martin had made me out to be. I was not the one deserving condemnation and shame—he was.

I knew by then that William Martin had never stopped lying about me. That fact had again opened the door to a lawsuit against him, and that was exactly what he was going to get from me. I had failed to stop him the first time, but *this* time, there would be no settlement or apology to recant. There would be only one thing for William Martin—a public trial by jury—and I would pursue it to the end, whatever that might be. If St. John's was harmed, or the individuals who controlled it were harmed or embarrassed, I no longer cared. The truth would be told no matter how hard they fought against it or what it cost me emotionally, physically or financially. But, it would not cost me spiritually because I knew, absolutely knew, that God would be with me regardless of the outcome.

There were two quotations I'd always sought to live by throughout my adult life. One was Polonius' advice to his son from Shakespeare's play, *Hamlet*, "This above all, to thine own self be true, and it shall follow as night the day, thou canst not then be false to any man." The other quotation is from Sir Edmund Burke, "The only thing necessary for Evil to triumph, is for good men to do nothing."

I resolved to be true to myself, and I resolved that I would not let Evil triumph because I chose to do nothing. I would have to find an attorney who believed as I did and who also believed *me*, one who had the courage to take on a priest, a church, and a powerful diocese, and who also had the knowledge and skill to prevail against them in spite of the odds against our winning.

# CHAPTER TWELVE

# Deliver Us From Evil

Before I could hire an attorney, I had to deal with the fact that I had signed a document stating that I would not sue Fr. Martin. However, because he had publicly recanted his admission of guilt, I believed I was no longer legally bound by the agreement. On November 1, 2005, one week after the spectacle on the steps of St. John's, I wrote a letter to Andy Swartz:

"This is to advise you that the certain 'Mutual Release' dated March 4, 2005, between your client, William Martin and me, Rayn Random, is no longer valid or binding. That agreement has been rendered null and void by William Martin. He has publicly recanted the admission he made in that agreement. I am no longer bound by the agreement or any of its terms and/or conditions. Any effort you may undertake on his behalf to enforce the agreement will expose, once again, that William Martin cannot be believed, as either one or the other of his public statements is most certainly a lie, inasmuch as they cannot both be true."

I received no reply. It was hard to imagine that Mr. Swartz couldn't think of anything to say in rebuttal. I had to believe the reason was that I was right. If he could have challenged my claim or argued that the agreement was still in effect, I'm quite sure he would have.

Writing to Swartz was the easy part. It was very satisfying to tell William Martin's arrogant apologist, who had referred to me in conversation with a friend of mine as "that crazy Rayn Random," that he no longer called the shots. The crucial and most difficult part was to find an attorney who had the competence and the courage to sue a priest, a church, and a diocese based on the word of a woman whose reputation and credibility had not only been totally trashed, but had been delivered to the county dump. I'd already experienced the fraternity brother mindset of Monterey's legal practitioners, and I also knew that no one around here would take my case because it might be bad for business, and no one wanted to take the risk of losing or associating with me. I had to find an attorney outside of Monterey County.

The quickest way to reach the greatest number of attorneys was to advertise, and so I placed an ad—a large one—in the San Francisco edition of the *Daily Journal,* a legal newspaper for lawyers in California. The ad ran every business day for a month without a single response. That was very discouraging and my conclusion was, although the ad was certainly noticed and read, it was clear that no one wanted to touch my case. Numerous times I had seen TV interviews with Gloria Allred, a Los Angeles attorney who mostly represents women, so I wrote to her, but never received a reply, not even a turndown.

Nothing was working. Added to that, I still hadn't heard from the district attorney's office whether or not they were going to prosecute me for criminal trespass, and I wondered what part Stephanie might be playing in their consideration. If she hadn't believed what Martin said about me, surely she would not have agreed to participate in my possible arrest, so she must have believed him. The fact that she had been on those church steps caused me great concern and anxiety, and I even wondered if she might be assigned to prosecute me. More than a month had gone by, and each time I phoned the Monterey Police Department, they said the District Attorney had the case. When I phoned the District Attorney's office, they told me they had no record of it and said the police department had it. I was beginning to think I couldn't trust any of them either, and I finally wrote directly to the District Attorney, Dean Flippo. He didn't reply personally, but his secretary was very responsive, and my concerns as to my case file's whereabouts were put to rest. At last, a report was issued which stated that the District Attorney's office had decided not to prosecute me because, "No rational jury would convict her." I was greatly relieved and especially welcomed the inclusion of the word "rational." That word had been in considerable disuse for quite a while.

I had just about given up ever finding anyone to take my case when, in December, a friend gave me the name of a Monterey attorney, Neil Shapiro. I reviewed his web site, and learned that he had been with a very prestigious San Francisco firm for many years, he had received numerous academic and professional awards, *and* he had been in Monterey for only three years. Maybe he hadn't joined the Monterey good old boys' and girls' club. Maybe there was hope. Then again, maybe I was wrong and it was only wishful thinking that anyone so accomplished would bother with my case.

I phoned his office, confident that I could persuade his secretary to schedule an appointment for me, even if she tried to put me off. To my horror, Neil Shapiro answered his own phone. That was a bad start because it was going to be too easy for him to turn me down. When he asked what my case was about, I suddenly didn't know where to begin, but I related things as best I could. Then I held my breath for the turn down. Instead, sounding slightly bemused, he said, "That sounds like an interesting change from my usual cases." We both laughed at the understatement, and he asked me when I wanted to come in. He hadn't said that he would take my case, but at least I still had a chance, and I was so relieved that he hadn't given me the same old attorney-speak answer about having "a heavy case load," that I almost cried.

When we met in his office, I was better prepared than I'd been over the phone, and we went through the case overview. As we talked, I was becoming optimistic that he would decide to represent me. In explaining my reasons for bringing the lawsuit, I quoted Polonius' advice. When I got to the second line, Mr. Shapiro finished it along with me. I knew then that I'd found the right attorney, and thankfully, he agreed to take my case.

In February 2006, the complaint against Martin was ready to be filed. I told Neil that I wanted to take it to the courthouse and file it myself. I couldn't help but smile as I waited in line for the clerk to stamp my papers with a case number and enter it into the court computer. I gave her a check for the filing fee, she looked over the papers, stamped them, kept the original, and handed the copies back to me. At last—for the first time in three years—I felt, once again, in control of what was going to happen in my life.

My friends, the four or five that were left, were happy for me too, but Carole warned me, "You'd better be careful because people are going to be very angry with you." I took that lightly and reassured her, "Fr. Martin wouldn't do anything. He's a coward." She gave me a stern look and said, "I don't mean Fr. Martin. I mean other church people. It doesn't have to be him." That was a sobering thought, and after that I used my alarm system conscientiously and worried about someone harming my German Shepherds or my cat. I had always taken the dogs with me when I went to church, and everyone at St. John's knew I had them and how important they were to me.

It turned out that Carole's advice was wise. The first moment of unease came through an encounter at the post office with a long time St. John's parishioner. He was an older gentleman, and I do mean gentleman in every way that I had ever observed. I met him as he was leaving and I was arriving. I expected a brief, friendly chat, but instead, after I said hello, he greeted me with a snarling, "What are you trying to prove?" Before I could say, "I'm trying to prove that I'm not the person Fr. Martin has made me out to be," he was gone. He'd left me standing in front of the post office with my mouth still open. I was shocked at that comment coming from a man whom I'd always regarded somewhat as a friend, who had been a guest in my home, who had the manners to write a charming thank-you note, and who once had said to me about Fr. Martin, "He lies very easily."

If that was *his* reaction, what must others at St. John's be thinking? And how crazy could some of their reasoning become in order to rid William Martin of the woman who was supposedly harming *his* reputation? They were bound to do something to harass me into giving up because that was exactly what both they and Martin had done to me before, only now the perceived threat to them was more serious.

Apparently, someone thought that flipping a circuit breaker at my house would send me a message, and during that second uneasy moment, I realized I was, indeed, being sent a warning because to do it, someone had avoided an electric gate. A tripped circuit breaker could happen any time, except that two years earlier I'd had two new banks of circuit breakers installed that provided a separate breaker for almost every electrical outlet in my house. And it had happened during daytime, when no lights were on and I wasn't at home using any appliances or TV.

That was followed by the discovery of a flat tire on my car, which was parked at the top of my long, steep driveway. Not even an extremely bored juvenile delinquent with nothing better to do would bother walking up my driveway just to let the air out of a tire. And then I recalled that earlier, a man who passed by my car had mentioned that one of my front tires appeared to be low. The Auto Club tow truck driver wasn't able to re-inflate the tire because the valve stem had been snapped off, and the odds of the stem breaking off by itself were remote. I knew it had been deliberately broken.

One morning when I backed my car down to the road, I became suspicious of two men sitting in a car parked near the foot of my driveway for no apparent reason. I live in the hills. We have no sidewalks, and people don't drive up here unless they have a specific reason or they live here. They certainly don't drive up to sit idly in their cars. The entire street is, at most, half a mile long and in the shape of a backward letter P. There is no connecting or cross-street, and the way out is the same as the way in. I turned right and was about to head down the hill, but when I noticed the parked car, a gut feeling told me to wait. I stopped, and in my rear view mirror, I took as good a look at the men as possible, and I purposely made my viewing of them very obvious. The men, a tall one behind the wheel and a shorter one next to him, sat perfectly still and looked straight back at me. I waited to see if they might get out of their car and go to a neighbor's house, as anyone normally would, but they just continued to sit in their car watching me, watching them. The man behind the wheel resembled a man from St. John's who had become a very familiar sight to me, but light was reflecting off their windshield and I couldn't be certain that it was he.

When I drove off, instead of going all the way down the hill, I made a quick right turn onto the loop of the "P" that would bring me back to my house in less than a minute and put me behind them. I drove as fast as I reasonably could, and felt the adrenalin kick in. When I got back to my driveway, the men had pulled away and were heading down the hill. Now they were in front of me. The hunters had become the hunted. They were in a hurry, probably believing that I'd recognized them, and I was close enough for them to see me in their rear view mirror. At each turn heading down the hill, I lost sight of them and each time they again came into view, they were still too far ahead for me to read their license number, which I desperately wanted. I'd stopped as briefly as I'd dared at the two stop signs on the way to the main road, knowing that once they reached it, I might lose them in traffic. When I got there, another car had already entered the space between us and, even worse, I had to stop for a particularly long red light, which gave them their escape to the freeway. Disappointing as that was, I at least had the satisfaction of putting a scare into them.

I'd had an instinctive, uneasy feeling for some time that I was being watched, and now I knew for certain. Those two were obviously amateurs or they wouldn't have gotten caught. That, however, made me stop and think that I could also be watched at any time by a professional, and then I wouldn't know it. It was a pretty sure thing that the defense attorneys were searching for everything and anything they could use to discredit me, or make me appear to be what William Martin claimed I was. Keeping an eye on my activities and who came to my house might prove to be informative for them, although I had nothing to hide.

Martin had only two legal defenses against my charge of defamation. Either he never said the things I claimed he did, or what he said about me was actually true. I had too many witnesses for him to successfully claim he'd never said those things, so his only other defense was to trash me with anything the attorneys could find in the hope they could convince a jury that what Martin said was true, and therefore he hadn't really damaged me. There were three defendants who had a lot to lose: William Martin, St. John's Chapel, and the Diocese of El Camino Real. There were three defense attorneys determined to win, and an insurance company that didn't want to pay a jury award. Clearly, they wanted to discover every possible nuance of my life, incriminating or not, and turn the most innocuous information into darkly suggestive reality for the jurors.

CHAPTER THIRTEEN

# Seek, and Ye Shall Find

The morning of May 3, 2006, was the opening round of pre-trial discovery, and I was the first person to be deposed. I was seated at a long table in a large rectangular room on the second floor of what used to be a house, but was now KC's Court Reporting. I was quietly waiting in anticipation of what was about to happen. Windows at one end of the room were open, letting in the fresh, springtime, ocean air that blended with the aroma of just-brewed coffee warming on a corner counter. A basket of mini-sized candy bars and packages of nuts was set in the middle of the table, the only piece of furniture in the room, except for the many chairs that surrounded it. My attorney, Neil Shapiro, sat on my left, and the court reporter sat on my right at the end of the table opposite the windows. I'd had my deposition taken a few years earlier on another matter and thought I knew what to expect, but this one would soon feel more like an inquisition.

The man who would later ask me if I was born "biologically female" was attorney Bryan Malone[24], representing Fr. Martin, and he sat across the table from me. He was one of three defense attorneys who were there to interrogate me in what turned out to be an almost ten-hour deposition. I had no notes and nothing to which I could refer during the questioning.

The church was represented by Andrew Swartz who had previously been, until the lawsuit was filed, Fr. Martin's personal attorney, and Anthony Lauria represented the diocese. It seemed to me that Mr. Swartz's switch of defendant clients was a conflict of interest, but if the other two parties didn't object, I had no reason

24    Later replaced by Michael LeVangie

to. All of them had been hired by the same insurance company that covered the defendants, who would suffer no financial losses. Only I took that risk.

I didn't recognize the only other woman in the room until I heard her say her name—Pamela Norton—and realized that she was the woman who had been standing outside the church in that cold Sunday morning drizzle, watching and waiting for me to arrive, so that she could advise me that I was trespassing and had to leave. Back then she'd worn shapeless black pants and a coat over her stout figure. On this spring morning she wore pastel colors, becoming makeup, and a smile, as she pleasantly chatted with everyone, except me. Although a Roman Catholic and a very new St. John's member, she had quickly and surprisingly—by her own admission—been appointed as a vestry member by Fr. Martin prior to the time at which one becomes eligible to serve in that capacity, and she was representing St. John's. Fr. Martin was also allowed to attend the deposition on his own behalf, but he chose not to. His absence was no surprise to me.

When all the good-mornings and polite comments ended and everyone was ready, the court reporter turned to me and said, "Raise your right hand, please. Do you state, under penalty of perjury, the testimony you are about to give will be the truth, the whole truth, and nothing but the truth?" I gave the same answer everyone does, "Yes."

Attorney Swartz was the first to question me. Swartz is a short, pudgy man, sixty-something I would guess, with thinning blonde hair in one of the popular L'Oreal shades. Although we had exchanged letters and he'd drafted the agreement with Martin, we had actually never met until this day, nor had I ever seen him before.

He asked me to state my name, which prompted several other questions about the origin of my first name. And he made an issue of the fact that I had been an independent paralegal for eleven years. He inquired, almost accusingly, about my clients—

did I ever work for an attorney? Did I know how to do legal research? What did I specialize in? Was I still doing paralegal work? Did I ever take the California bar exam? If he looked in the Monterey phone book under paralegals, would he find my name? At the time, that all seemed irrelevant as I was represented by an outstanding attorney and was completely unequipped to represent myself in this kind of case.

Attorney Malone showed an even greater interest in my name than Swartz had. He was the youngest and tallest of the three, probably in his early forties, and seemed to be the most open and friendly. He was remarkably well groomed with perfectly-coiffed black hair, and he appeared to take excellent care of himself. I was prepared to like him, if one can actually *like* an opposing attorney. That is, until he asked, "And I mean no disrespect by this. But were you born biologically female?" I quickly changed my mind about liking him.

When I answered yes, it surprised me that my answer wasn't good enough to settle the question because he then inquired if I had ever been considered for transsexual, or any other type of gender identity surgery. I was shocked. The first question had been insulting enough, and if he'd dared to ask that same question of a man, he probably would have gotten a hard look that warned him to back off, and that one reply would have been sufficient. The second question might have gotten him a fist in his face. Not having that option, I replied that I had not been a candidate for a sex change.

But, he still wasn't finished. He followed with, "Has anyone, other than Fr. Martin, ever said that you were a man and not a woman, to your knowledge?" I said "No," and then it was back to my first name again. I answered those questions by telling him that it was my given name, my father had chosen it for me, and occasionally I got junk mail addressed to Ryan because someone thought Rayn was a misspelling and "corrected" it. In answer to his next questions, I said that I didn't know if anyone at St. John's was confused by my name and thought I might be a man, and no one had ever asked me. Just when I thought that question was the most bizarre of all, he followed with, "Same question with respect to 'Ray' and then the 'N' being your middle initial." I struggled to keep from shaking my head in disbelief and wondered what went on in this man's brain. I couldn't believe that he was serious, but of course, he was, and so I answered his question.

Malone continued, "Okay. I believe you said earlier you have not had plastic surgery." I had been asked that question more than once, and I had answered, "No," each time. Here it came again—and there went my patience.

Before he could pose the question, I looked straight at him and said firmly, "No, I have not. I do not have implants." He gave me a weak little smile and said, "That's right where I was going to go."

I'd had my gender questioned to the point that it was now intentional harassment, and it was coming from two men who had made themselves totally disgusting. I couldn't let on that I was annoyed, but my thoughts were private, and Malone was so hung up on my possible gender change that I couldn't help but wonder about him. He was a master of fastidious page-turning with the tips of his delicate, white fingers, his little finger had the perfect tea-time crook, and he kept his lips sweetly pursed. I mentally smiled at the thought of him in a courtroom, examining his client, William Martin, on the witness stand. They would have made quite a pair. While I waited for his next question, I'd hoped that I wouldn't have to answer the same ones again. But, he still didn't give up and continued with, "Have you ever told anyone at St. John's that you were considering implantation surgery?" He just couldn't bring himself to let go of the subject, and it was beyond offensive.

My pre-trial deposition was sleazier than I could ever have anticipated. The spectacle of three middle-aged men, leaning forward in their chairs, intently asking probing, personal, adolescent schoolboy questions of a woman about her gender, anatomy, and name, in a charade effort to discover what could *not* be discovered by asking questions of her, was repulsive. A simple test, in use for decades, would have spared me the insults from these repugnant men and their crude questioning. Wearing expensive suits did not negate the "creep" factor.

Whether or not my breasts were false was easily provable by an inquiry to my gynecologist. That, of course, would immediately prove that Martin had lied. They couldn't let that happen, so instead, they argued that it was no big deal that he had said it, the same way that Swartz and Gordon had argued that leaving out the apology was no big deal. It was a big deal to me because it implied a possible intimacy that didn't exist, and it supported his claim that I was a man, which in itself would be a terrible insult to *any* woman, well, almost any woman. The defense attorneys' puerile efforts to "discover" the truth would have been laughable if they hadn't been so revolting.

The hot tub was more raw meat that they relished ripping into. The portrait they wanted to paint of me was as a sex-crazed woman—or man—in shameless, hot pursuit of an innocent young[25] priest. If they were able to convince a jury that I had a damaged reputation to begin with, it would refute my claim that it was harmed by what Martin said. As for the phone calls, they could have subpoenaed the records, all of which were available. I had made only one phone call to William Martin a few days after our February 28, 2003 party and never made another. They probably already had the records, as they didn't press that issue.

Martin was never able to describe any "inappropriate advances," so he blamed that idea on Frank Reynolds, who turned out to be a fortuitous scapegoat. Frank had since suffered a stroke and could not have contradicted Martin. Had Frank been able to respond, he most certainly would not have accepted the blame. Howard Sitton might *still* throw himself on his sword for Martin,

---

25    43 years old

but Frank would have too much respect for the truth and for himself.

The restraining order never existed, and court records show that none had ever been applied for. They already knew what a lie that was.

The most Martin ever admitted, outside of the settlement agreement, was that he had said at least one time, to one person, that I had made him "uncomfortable by suggesting that" he join me in my hot tub. In the five or six times he claimed that happened, he was never able to describe what I'd said or done, or where I had done it.

In spite of admitting in the agreement that he had said all of those things, in his deposition and interrogatory responses he now denied saying *any* of them. And then, just to make it all really, really clear that he never, never, ever said them, he came up with a new story—it was the St. John's *congregation* that had said them—to *each other.*

In Martin's sworn deposition, Shapiro asked, "...you agreed to sign language saying, I made these statements and I apologize for them, right?"

The answer Martin gave was incomprehensible. He said, "Yes. This...this paragraph for me was indicative of—of something that had reached her through whatever means and inflicted a wound on her part. And so I—I have to be held responsible for this. That is my thought process. That is why I am bound by this. That is also why this agreement is not an agreement of finality and closure. It is the possibility within it of an openness for reconciliation. I mean, I don't want to hurt Rayn Random, and there's been a lot of talk in my church and a lot of gossip and a lot of horrible things that people have said to one another and they are nothing but instances of hurt and maliciousness. And I have no intention of hurting Rayn and we had a very good friendship and I admit fully that, you know, perhaps, you know, in the past at times I was indeed, you know, not mature enough to deal with just what she said in her letter, you know, affection. I admit that. And, you know, after all of this, I mean, it's very interesting to me and I'm thinking about this and, you know, I—I—there were absolutely many, many beautiful gifts that she has brought to us, and I'm not closing the door on the possibility that she can bring them back."

What? When he'd finished speaking, he looked across the table at me, leaned forward, and with an expression of painful sincerity, said, "I mean, I'm not interested in hurting you, Rayn. I'm not." It was an absolutely disgusting performance after the years he'd spent destroying everything I had been. Protocol prevented any response from me.

Martin continued, seeming to now blame *me* for failing to seek reconciliation with *him*. "I signed this agreement in order to allow the possibility of an amicable reconciliation apart from any spiritual means to reconciliation which were not pursued by Rayn Random at that time. However, the reconciliation statement was still a reconciliation statement and I left open the possibility of future spiritual reconciliation. This was the only means I felt that I had in order to keep the door open and in order to offer the fact that she must in theory and in practice, as I must in theory and in practice, allow for reconciliation between us. I felt that this was what I had to do in order to express my sorrow to her. *And there is nothing in here that said that she couldn't come back to St. John's.*"

I didn't have the faintest idea of the "reconciliation statement" he kept referring to. But his contention that he kept the door open and expressed his sorrow was absolutely mind-blowing. Did that mean that Monica Nathan, Pamela Norton and Howard Sitton would have immediately stepped aside and ushered me into a pew on that drizzly, cold Sunday morning if I'd said, "I came to reconcile with Fr. Martin?" Sitton would probably have interpreted that as a ruse for me to get close enough to physically attack Martin, and that would have sent him into hysterical defense mode to protect his leader.

When Shapiro questioned if Martin had asked anyone to tell me to leave St. John's, Martin answered, "No, sir." When Shapiro asked, "Did you know before she appeared for services in early March (just after the agreement) that her entrance would be blocked and she would be asked to leave," Martin's answer was, "Yes."

When Shapiro then asked him if he had been a party to the conversation during which the decision was made to prevent my entering St. John's, Martin said, "Yes, sir."

His answer was right out of a scene from Shakespeare where King Henry II laments, "Will no one rid me of this meddlesome priest?" Only, this time it was the priest doing the lamenting, and William Martin didn't have to "ask" anyone to get rid of me anymore than King Henry had to "ask" his knights to get rid of Thomas Becket, Archbishop of Canterbury. Becket was slain by four knights who understood Henry's unspoken request and consequently attacked and killed Becket with their swords in 1011, while Becket was at the altar of the Canterbury Cathedral. My attackers consisted of only three who kept me *from* the altar. Instead of swords, they used their razor-edged tongues and blind, misguided devotion to a man they never questioned—just as King Henry's knights never questioned him. However, Henry later chose to do penance for the crime he prompted. William Martin did nothing, except claim his "sorrow"—under pressure— but, not for anything *he* had done.

Shapiro went through our list of witnesses and asked Martin, one by one, if he had ever said to anyone the comments he admitted to in the Settlement Agreement. Martin was supposed to either admit or deny each statement. He answered every statement question, "No." Then, to make absolutely certain, Shapiro asked as to each statement, "Did you tell *anyone?*" Martin's answer was, "No."

Shapiro quoted a previous statement of Martin's: "I signed this document in good faith, and as is demanded in the Christian church, it was my responsibility as shepherd to bear the burden of sins committed through the gossip and hearsay of members of my flock." Asked what gossip and hearsay, Martin said, "The gossip and hearsay that I assume led to the communication of the cruel statements to Rayn Random." He said he assumed the gossip came from members of his "flock" because he was told "that people were gossiping about—certain people had been gossiping about Rayn Random." The person he claimed gave him that information was, of course, Frank Reynolds, the one person who could not rebut him.

Shapiro's last question was, "You in fact, entered into the agreement because you wanted to 'avoid litigation and publicity.' Isn't that true?"

Martin's answer was as evasive as ever: "That was not my thought. I just know that it's not—it wasn't about ultimate litigation and publicity. It was about, you know, frustration and pain. And I think that it was honestly, I think that it was—I mean, I think—I think I was confused and I think—obviously I didn't want litigation and publicity but I also didn't want further frustration and pain, and I knew that we could not and I would not shut the door on any possibility of reconciliation, and I was sorrowful for what had been said."

Martin's was just one of the depositions that we took, and some of the answers we got from the others were as bizarre as his had been. We deposed most of the witnesses we intended to call and the witnesses we were reasonably certain the defense would call. The three defense attorneys had the right to cross examine every witness we deposed, and Martin had the option to attend each deposition but, he still chose not to come to any of them. Pamela Norton, representing St. John's, attended every one and presumably reported to Martin. She and I never spoke to each other, except for a general "good morning" addressed to everyone in the room. I had no cause, nor reason, to show her any courtesy and had no intention of appearing to do so. The only memorable impression about Ms. Norton's presence, except for her strange testimony, was that she made distracting noises by opening the crinkly packages of candy and nuts while others were testifying, and we could hear her chewing every bite.

In her own deposition Shapiro asked her, "At the time you read (the settlement agreement), did you believe that William Martin had made those statements about Ms. Random?" She said that she believed it. When Shapiro followed by asking if she ever talked to Martin about "what he had said about Ms. Random," she replied, "No. I was too embarrassed."

Shapiro followed with, "But, when you read this, you understood that William Martin had said all of the things set forth in paragraph 1?" Her answer was, "Right." Asked if it had troubled her, she said it had. As to whether Martin should then continue as rector of a Church if he'd said those things about a parishioner, she matter-of-factly replied, "Yes."

Did she think the parishioner should be excluded from the church? She said, "I felt—yes." To clarify her answer beyond a doubt, Shapiro summarized by asking, "You felt that although Fr. Martin had made false and derogatory statements about a parishioner and then admitted it, the parishioner should go and he should stay?" Again, Ms. Norton said, "Yes."

Then, for a brief moment, she seemed about to change course when Shapiro asked her, "Why?" She said, in a very serious and thoughtful manner, "I just feel he should be held to a higher standard," I held my breath in expectation of a turnaround until she continued, "and that even though he may have made a *mistake,* you know, I just feel that he was—he was to be forgiven and he should be allowed to stay, and the parishioner should go. That's how I felt at the time."

Shapiro asked, "Do you still feel that way?" Ms. Norton said firmly, "Yes, I do."

However, she acknowledged—without the slightest embarrassment or apology—that *she had no understanding as to why the parishioner had to go* and, not surprisingly, she never asked anyone to tell her why.

Monica Nathan was the other woman who had blocked my entry into church, and she also signed the vestry letter telling me to never return. I had not seen her before except in the drizzle outside the church. In her testimony she said that she had been in the Army for twenty years. Her rank when she retired was Lieutenant Colonel, and she had been an operating nurse with clinical and management duties. She was currently employed as a peri-operative nurse and quality assurance coordinator. I was impressed by her credentials and considering her military background, I expected her to have excellent recall and knowledge.

Neil asked: "On that occasion (the church steps) did you, or either of the other people with you, tell Ms. Random that the congregation had voted to exclude her?"

Ms. Nathan responded, "I don't recall saying those words or hearing those words said."

When Shapiro followed with, "In fact, did the congregation ever vote on whether or not Ms. Random should be excluded," her answer was, "No," a complete contradiction of what Pamela Norton told me when I was barred from entry. And, just like Ms. Norton, Ms. Nathan never asked Fr. Martin if his admission that he made the statements was true, nor did she ever ask anyone else. It was stunning to learn that no one ever asked William Martin about the statements he made, or wondered *why* they were all being asked to do such horrible things to a fellow church member. Howard Sitton repeatedly said that he "just couldn't believe it." Apparently, if he couldn't believe it, it couldn't be true, or even worthy of question or investigation.

It was becoming clear to me that St. John's Chapel had been turned into a personality cult. No one wanted to know the truth or admit, even to themselves, that the person they so blindly followed was a fraud. It was sounding more and more like the People's Temple that Jim Jones created in San Francisco, which was applauded and rewarded by politicians and city leaders until his believers followed him en masse to the jungle in Guyana where, on Jones' orders, 918 men, women and children died from consuming a poisoned drink. I hoped that William Martin stuck with soup making and wouldn't branch out. He referred to the parishioners as his "flock" and he was their shepherd, but it was supposed to be only a figurative reference, not a literal one to them as sheep, but that's exactly what they had become.

To my great surprise, Ms. Nathan claimed to remember almost nothing of the previous four years, recent events, discussions, and even that she was present at meeting that had taken place only four days earlier. Questioning her was an exercise in futility. She said, "I don't recall" so many times that I wondered if she would be able to find her way home because she had probably already forgotten where she lived.

Unlike Ms. Nathan, Howard Sitton not only remembered *everything*, he wrote much of it down in detail, and that propensity prompted a comment from William Martin when he was presented with a document written by Howard. Martin said, "You know, Howard writes a lot, and Howard sends a lot of emails and letters to me, and I have to confess to you that sometimes I don't read everything that he sends because it's verbose." He thought a moment and quickly added, "Anyway, maybe you don't need to put that in there (the transcript)."

In his report of the Sunday when he accosted me by the side door path after the service and asked me to leave, Howard wrote, "I went towards her per your instructions[26]... and said, 'Ms. Random, Fr. Martin is going to be coming out this way and does not want to meet with you and wants you to leave.'" He did add a little humor to his report, although I'm sure that he, himself, took his words very seriously. He wrote to Martin, "As I indicated to you I would, I remained just inside or outside the parish hall side door so as to be able to accompany you should

---

26      Martin claimed not to remember his instructions

you wish to come into the hall and have someone between you and Random." *Howard the Hero!* It sounds like a Saturday morning cartoon show, and from my observation that day, it even looked like one. The announcer would have said, "Stay tuned boys and girls to see how Howard the Hero faithfully defends his priest against a treacherous, evil woman who is lurking inside the church, disguised in a hat, drinking coffee, and pretending to chat with parishioners while secretly waiting for the right moment to launch a ferocious assault against a holy man of the cloth who is dedicated only to spreading God's message of love."

We continued with depositions and preparations for trial, but we still had not been given a date or assigned a judge. By the time the date was announced—February 26, 2007—I was already looking forward to it, even though it was still months away. Everything else in my life had been put on hold. As with almost everyone who is a party to a lawsuit, it was never out of my mind, and there was never any way to predict or guess the outcome. I'd known from the beginning that the odds were against me, but I never regretted making the choice to seek vindication by a jury trial. If I had given up, I knew I would regret it later when it would be too late. I could accept losing, provided I had given it my best effort. The trial would be difficult, frightening, have an unpredictable result, and I knew from the beginning that it would be expensive, but I had to take the risk. When I ran out of savings, I used the equity line against my house, and if I lost, I had no idea what I would do to recover. I might have to finally do what my dinner guest had said she would have done rather than stay and fight—sell my house and leave town. I would never choose to do that, but if I lost, that's what it would likely come to. But—I'd still have my self respect and for me, that was priceless.

Part of the reason it was so costly was that Neil was up against three other attorneys of record and at least two more behind the scenes. Sometimes one side in a lawsuit will file so many documents with the court that the opposing party runs out of money just responding to them. I don't claim that it happened in my case, but the defense generated a lot of paperwork that required our responses and court appearances for Neil. Fortunately for me, I never once needed to question any charge, and when I phoned or emailed Neil, unless it was a very lengthy case discussion, he never billed me. He never kept me waiting beyond the same day for a response, and often it was immediate. I doubt that any client ever had a more considerate attorney, or a better working attorney/client relationship. The credit goes to Neil.

As our trial date approached, we were also nearing a deadline for completion of our discovery proceedings. Anything after that date had to be argued by both sides and decided by the judge as to its admissibility. We had taken thirteen depositions. The Defense took only one—mine.

In December of 2006, I had been out shopping in the afternoon and as usual, had taken my dogs with me in the car. I was returning home and only a few blocks away from my house when I got a call on my cell phone from the alarm company. They said the alarm was going off in my house, and the police were on their way. My immediate thought was that perhaps I hadn't tightly closed a door and it had blown open. I was almost home and it was still daylight, so I thought it couldn't be anything serious. I told them to cancel the call to the police.

When I started up my driveway, I could hear the alarm and the blaring, urgent sound immediately drowned out my earlier casual attitude. I thought that perhaps I shouldn't have been so quick to cancel the police. I let the dogs out of the car when I reached the top of my driveway and waited while they sniffed the ground the way they often do for deer or raccoon scent, but they didn't seem unusually excited, so we went to the house. After I unlocked the door, I let them in first while I paused in the doorway. As I glanced around, nothing seemed any different from the way I'd left it, so I stepped inside and shut off the alarm.

After I'd visually checked through the house, I phoned the alarm company to tell them everything seemed to be alright. But, it wasn't. The alarm company said *someone had been in my house* and that person, or those persons, had tripped the alarm outside my office door three times. It's not possible for my cat or my dogs to ever trip that alarm because it's at shoulder height, is heat sensitive, and can only be set off by someone walking past it.

There are two ways to set the alarm system. One setting is for times when people are at home, and the other is for times that no one is home. When the alarm is set for no one at home and an outside door is opened, the alarm starts a countdown. If a correct security code is entered on the alarm key pad within a time limit, nothing happens and the system shuts off. If no code is entered, the alarm will eventually sound off. However, the count down is long enough that someone could have come into the house and walked to my office before it ended. But, once someone reached my office door, the heat sensor would immediately set off the alarm, which is exactly what happened. There would still be sufficient time between the alarm sounding, the company calling my home, then the police, and finally calling me on my cell phone, for whoever it was inside to get away before encountering me coming up the hill, or the arrival of the police. The system has since been reconfigured to operate differently, in case of a return visit.

In spite of my wanting to disbelieve it, there was no refuting that someone had come into my house and had reached my office, which is where I keep all of my files and records—and my computer. During my deposition I was asked more than thirty questions, at four separate times, about my computer. It was also possible that the purpose for getting into my house might have been to tap my phone or to plant a hidden camera or listening device, so I called a private investigator to check into it. My house and phones were clean, and I was very relieved because if the phone were tapped, all of my conversations with Neil about our case could be heard and recorded. Once again, that uneasy feeling of being observed returned.

Near the end of January, almost a year after the lawsuit had been filed, the trial was postponed until June 18, 2007 so that Mr. Swartz could go to Hawaii. Four more months was a long time to wait when we'd come so close to our original date. While we were waiting for June, there were motion hearings for the attorneys and settlement conferences, for which both Martin and I had to appear, along with our attorneys, although we didn't have to testify. William Martin always had an entourage of supporters from St. John's and a number of other churches from around the diocese. The only two people on my side for our appearances were Neil and me. When Neil was in chambers, I sat by myself and got the usual looks of disgust and contempt that seemed to be asking, why doesn't this dreadful woman stop harassing this poor priest? I knew why, and I knew that they would find out when the truth was told.

We also had a court ordered mediation conference in a neutral Monterey attorney's office. We first met all together in one room so the attorney could explain his mediation procedure before separating us into two groups. There was a table that accommodated four people, and Neil and I sat on one side. The room kept filling up with more and more people arriving on behalf of Martin, who sat directly across from me, sideways so he didn't have to face me. There were at least ten people who came with him and they were lined shoulder-to-shoulder against the wall behind him. The scene summed up the situation—two against eleven, or more. The result of that meeting was that the three defendants jointly offered five thousand dollars as settlement. It was too ridiculous to even laugh at.

Neil later received an offer of $20,000, and the suggestion that Martin would leave town. It was another insulting offer and didn't come close to covering my costs, even to that point. Besides, I was not seeking money, I wanted my reputation back. If

I had settled for *any* amount, then the story circulated would have been, "The poor man had to pay her off, *again!* I didn't care in the least what William Martin did. Neil's reply to them was, "I don't believe Ms. Random cares whether he stays or goes."

The three defendants made no further offers, and I was glad that they didn't. From then on it was just a matter of mentally counting the days until our court date. Neil had many other cases that demanded his time, and I had things to take care of as well, but I still had more than enough time for mental excursions into various possibilities and outcomes. One concern I had was that there would be another postponement. There were many potential causes that could have made one necessary. The judge or one of the attorneys might become ill, or have a serious family emergency. That would knock us off the calendar and we would have another long wait to get back on.

The week before our trial date, everything seemed to be in its proper, secure place and we were ineluctably headed to the almost "High Noon" climax that would determine my future. Whether or not we would prevail felt, to me, as though it had already been pre-determined. But, I didn't know what that determination was. I never prayed to God that we would win. I said what I had learned in Sunday school as a child: "Thy will be done." What I did ask of God was, "please give me strength and courage."

# CHAPTER FOURTEEN

# And He Shall Come to Judge

The night before the trial started, my biggest fear was that I would set my alarm wrong, or I wouldn't sleep all night and be late for court. I worried that even if I arrived on time, I wouldn't find a parking place, or I'd be so sleep deprived that I couldn't concentrate on the people and the situation that held the key to my future. Thankfully, my fears were unfounded. I did sleep, I did find a parking place, and it was a little before nine when I arrived.

The court building is situated on a hill, and the vista is spectacular from the second floor where our assigned courtroom and the law library are located. But, even though I've often stopped to enjoy the view, it was the last thing on my mind this day. On the first floor, every area was crowded with people in line at the metal detector, or conversing in small groups, waiting for the courtrooms to be opened. They were prospective jurors, attorneys, and spectators, not only for my case, but for others scheduled to begin that day.

The second floor was equally crowded, and when I stepped out of the elevator, I was met with dozens of curious eyes. I recognized some of the people from St. John's and needless to say, there were no smiles from them. Most of the others, I concluded, were potential jurors. As I looked at them, they were looking at me and creating their first impression of the woman who had caused them to miss work and had called them to a situation they probably would have preferred to avoid.

Prospective jurors came from all over Monterey County. The Peninsula, itself, is limited in size by the surrounding ocean, but the rest of the county is large. There are small rural towns, the beautiful, black-dirt, farming communities of the Salinas River Valley—which was the setting for John Steinbeck's *Grapes of Wrath*—and the mostly Hispanic City of Salinas, the County Seat of Monterey. Looking at the potential jurors, I thought that a computer could not have selected a more diverse group from the county's half million residents. It covered every locale, from posh Pebble Beach to farms and ranches, every age, student to retired, every education level, and every color of the human rainbow.

Everyone was waiting for the bailiff to open the courtroom and when he did, it couldn't accommodate all of the people and those who were not potential jurors or parties to the case were asked to, again, wait outside in the hall. Neil was already at the plaintiff's table, and the only place for me was a wooden, straight-backed chair behind him where I would sit throughout the entire eight days of the trial.

Looking at the courtroom from the entry doors on each side of a tiny vestibule, the judge's raised platform was at the far wall with the Great Seal of the State of California behind it and an American flag and a California State flag on each side. The court clerks sat lower down on the left, and the bailiff's desk was midway against the left wall. The three defense counsel sat together at two tables on the left. The raised witness box was on the right, next to the judge, the court reporter sat in front of the witness box on the right, and the jurors sat along the right wall. Neil was at a single table opposite the jury, and I was behind him. William Martin sat behind the three defense attorneys. A man I didn't know, but had seen previously—most likely on behalf of the diocese—sat on his left and Pamela Norton was to his right, about four or five feet from me, on my left.

The press had shown up, and there was a huge TV camera set up in the hallway, facing the courtroom doors. Each day in the *Monterey Herald,* the trial coverage was on the front page of the first or second section, almost always the top headline. There was some coverage on local TV news, but I didn't see any of it.

The Honorable Susan Dauphine was our assigned judge. She had not been our preference, but we had already used our one preemptory challenge on another judge who was a blatant misogynist. He later took early retirement from the bench while disciplinary charges were pending against him regarding vile comments he made about a lesbian judge in Los Angeles, and inappropriate statements he made to his female clerk. Monterey had only four civil court judges. One was on vacation, the judge being investigated had not been replaced, the third was a very qualified and experienced woman we would have been glad to have, but she was unavailable, and the fourth was Judge Dauphine. We didn't know what to expect from her, but we found out very quickly.

Right from the beginning, Dauphine repeatedly ruled against us in chambers as to what evidence she would allow us to present to the jury. The three defense attorneys argued against almost everything in order to protect their clients, and she repeatedly sided with their arguments to the extent that we had almost no evidence left to present. Our entire case had been so shredded by her pre-trial rulings that Neil suggested to me—"She may as well issue a Summary Judgment in favor of the defendants before we even go to trial." Her rulings seemed to be her personal choices, not what the California Rules of Evidence entitled us to.

One afternoon while I was working out at Spanish Bay several months before trial, there had been only three of us in the weight room, and I couldn't help but hear the conversation between the two men who were near me. One of them had recently had shoulder surgery and was just getting back to playing tennis. He mentioned to the second man how pleased he was with the outcome, and he had great praise for the surgeon.

Their conversation continued and soon after, the second man commented that Judge Dauphine was an excellent and avid tennis player, but that many of her opponents privately disputed her line calls.[27] At the time, I chalked it up to frustrated losers, but now, seeing what she was doing to our evidence, I wondered if Judge Dauphine wasn't doing the same thing *in* the court as *on* the court. Was she intentionally ruling things the way that she personally wanted them to be, instead of what the Rules of Evidence stated? And then, the inevitable question was why would she do that? What personal interest could she possibly have in this case? I'd been informed that one of the attorneys who had declined my case was a good friend of the vacationing judge, and had told the judge that he thought mine was a "bad case." Had Dauphine already decided, too, that we had a "bad case?" But, even if she had, her personal opinions were irrelevant and we were entitled to fair and impartial legal rulings—which we were not getting.

My first view of Judge Dauphine was when she appeared from a side door after the bailiff called out, "All rise, the honorable Judge …".and she stepped up to the bench.

She wore a black robe, of course, but I didn't realize how very petite she was until I later saw her step down from the bench during our first recess and stand next to other people. She was sixty-something, wore her very blonde hair in a shoulder length pageboy style, and from a distance, appeared attractive.

That first day of trial did not bode well, and it appeared that everyone—including Judge Dauphine—with the exception of the potential jurors, had already chosen a side. The gallery was no different. Apparently everyone who had a clerical collar in his wardrobe had also arrived to support the Reverend William Martin in his hour of tribulation. The future of one of their own was on trial, and they all showed up. And, I do mean *show*ed up. They made such an obnoxious spectacle of themselves, strutting around, chatting with each other in a superiorly confident manner,

---

27    A friend who played at the same club confirmed that other players privately questioned her calls, and that she had also witnessed questionable calls made by Dauphine.

and continually creating a disturbance by entering and leaving the courtroom that Judge Dauphine complained. The next day, most of the clerical collars had been replaced by shirts and ties, so the cheering squad didn't stand out so much. The gang from St. John's was there to support their leader, sitting excitedly behind me in the front visitors' row and eager for the start of my final rejection by all of society. Whenever I turned around, I was immediately met by their collective smirks only two feet away from my face. Gladys Shultz seemed especially excited. If I'd arrived in a tumbrel at the French guillotine, they could hardly have been more bright-eyed with anticipation.

Because of all the motions and arguments remaining before the court regarding what evidence would be admissible, jury selection didn't begin until the second day. By Tuesday morning, Judge Dauphine had finally admitted just enough evidence for us to proceed. I felt a little better about her and hoped our worries that she was biased against us were over, but just before the second day ended, I would be jolted by news that proved me wrong—our worries had only begun.

At 10:14 AM, all prospective jurors were sworn to tell the truth, and voir dire—questioning by the attorneys—began. By the lunch break, many potential jurors had been questioned and excused, and over half of the fourteen (two alternates) that we needed had been seated in the jury box. During the noon recess, the bailiff closed the courtroom to everyone except the attorneys and the parties, so that the court could hear, off the record, from two people who had been selected, but had pressing reasons to be excused. After hearing their reasons, all parties agreed to excuse both of them.

Finally, after more consultation and questioning, a jury panel of 12, plus the two alternates, was sworn at 2:58 PM. on our second day of trial. The jurors were given their preliminary instructions by the judge and excused until 9:00 am the following day.

During the following recess, a woman who had been observing the trial since the beginning and had introduced herself to me earlier, told me something that shocked me beyond anything I could have imagined. She revealed that Judge Dauphine had a son who was a third year seminary student, studying to become *a priest*. I felt the blood drain from my head and a knot in my stomach. *Judge Dauphine had withheld critical information that she was ethically obliged to disclose.* That opinion is unanimous among everyone who has heard about it, including attorneys.

Neil's reaction was one of absolute shock and disbelief, made even worse in light of her evidence rulings against us. I no longer doubted that she wanted us to lose, even before a single word of evidence had been presented to the jury. Now I *knew* in my sinking heart that Neil was faced with not just three opposing attorneys, but *four*. They were the three attorneys of record, and the "Honorable" Judge Susan Dauphine. With no preemptory challenge left, we could only get rid of her for cause. Neil said that disqualifying her was hardly a sure thing. It would be a well-deserved public humiliation for Dauphine if she were removed from the case at that stage of the trial—made even worse by disclosure of the cause—but she would argue against her removal and insist that she could give us a fair trial. She had already given Neil that exact same argument in her chambers when he confronted her privately with what we'd discovered. Most likely, the presiding judge would agree with Dauphine and *then* we'd end up with a judge who not only didn't like our case from the very beginning and had a serious conflict of interest, but one who would be infuriated with us throughout the entire trial. Even an unsuccessful attempt to have her removed would certainly make the news, and if we did succeed in having her discharged, we would have further problems. Getting assigned another judge would not be simple and we'd have to wait months longer for a new trial date that all parties would be available for. I couldn't have taken another delay emotionally, or financially.

We had no choice but to keep her, and hope that she would deliver the fair trial she'd promised. It was a dreadfully uneasy feeling to know that after all I had staked on the truth being told, *I couldn't trust the judge who had the power to determine what evidence and what testimony the jury would be allowed to hear.* Her smiles at all who sat beneath her, and her over-acted graciousness betrayed the dishonesty that I saw behind the façade she presented. To me, she was the DIS-honorable Judge Dauphine.

On Wednesday, day three, after more discussions between the court and the attorneys, the jury was brought in at 9:12am. Court reporter's notes state, "Discussions are had between the court and jurors regarding The Monterey *Herald's* article dated June 20," which had appeared that morning. The headline read: "Episcopal Priest on trial for slander." The story, written by Virginia Hennessey opened with:

"Slander, stalking and trans-sexuality. It's not what you'd expect when the local Episcopal priest goes on trial. But it is what jurors in a Monterey courtroom will hear beginning this morning. Attorneys will present opening statements in the trial of the Rev. William Martin, pastor of St. John's Chapel Episcopal Church in Monterey, who is accused of defaming former parishioner Rayn Random." Hennessey continued:

"In pretrial rulings, Judge Susan Dauphine said Random would not be allowed to admit evidence regarding those actions (denial of Communion and the letter from Bishop Shimpfky) because they were 'ecclesiastic' decisions. Left unclear on Tuesday was whether jurors would be told that church officials subsequently called Monterey police and had Random removed from the premises for 'trespassing.' Dauphine said that action was not an ecclesiastical decision and could be admissible."

*But, after Judge Dauphine stated that she would allow that evidence, she made certain that it would be impossible for us to get it in.*

Hennessey continues:

"However, she said, it would be difficult for Shapiro to put it in context without telling jurors that Random had been ejected from church membership." Judge Dauphine was not about to let the jurors know that I had been ejected from membership at St. John's or denied Communion.

The article is lengthy, but Ms. Hennessey concludes with:

"In a courtroom already packed with potential jurors, the hearing attracted more than a dozen observers, including other local Episcopal clergy. At one point, Dauphine grew so irritated with the noise that she forbid anyone from entering or exiting the courtroom while attorneys were questioning the panelists. The courtroom will be open to the public today."

There was one more matter that had to be taken up before opening statements could be heard. A juror who had already been sworn in, privately asked to be excused because she feared possible retaliation against her grandchild, who attended an Episcopal school. If the final decision were 12-0 in my favor, it would be obvious that she voted against the priest, the church, and the diocese. Even if it were a hung jury or a mixed verdict, the jurors would be polled and she would have to declare in open court how she voted. She wanted to protect her grandchild from the power of the church to punish, and I understood that—perfectly. She was excused and replaced by one of the two alternate jurors, leaving only one.

Opening statements came after that. Neil was first, and following is part of his statement to the jurors:

"Her reputation probably will never be the same as it had been for 60-some years before all these statements were made. She has endured four years of tears and pain and has prayed a great deal trying to get past what I think anyone would understand as a devastating experience.

"If not for her good friends, I'm not sure she would have made it that far.

"The key question in front of you in this case essentially is who is telling the truth. I read to you what William Martin admitted saying. Now he says he never said any of those things. Except he does admit the hot tub statement, but he says it's true." Shapiro read the list of things Martin said and then denied.

"You will hear testimony from a veritable parade of witnesses who will contradict exactly what I just read to you. You will hear from Joan Fontaine, Jo Howard, Kim Rennick, Anita Steel, Clifford Bagwell, John Steel, Dale Howard, Walter Alsky. Each of them will testify under oath that they heard from the mouth of William Martin one or more of the very statements he swears he never made. Ultimately, you will have to decide who is telling the truth, him or all of them."

Following Shapiro's remarks, Mr. Swartz stood to deliver his opening statement. He wore a suit and tie, and his fresh looking baby skin and rosy cheeks made him look like the Pillsbury dough boy—all dressed up—except for his phony smile as he greeted the jurors. I realized, as I watched him begin his performance, that a courtroom is actually a theatre, a stage for not only the presentation of facts, but for the portrayal of emotions, some genuine and others just theatrical illusion. The judge is the director, the attorneys and witnesses are the actors, the gallery is the audience, and the jurors are the critics. The symbol for theatre—the smiling mask and the tragic mask—is just as appropriate to the courtroom as it is to the theatrical arts.

After greeting the jury, Mr. Swartz, acting as his own stage hand, placed an easel in front of me and set a huge color blowup photo of St. John's Chapel in front of my face. It blocked my view of everyone except him when he was on the side of the easel facing the jurors, and I could still see Pamela Norton and William Martin to my left. No one could see me, and it was as though I were no longer present, which was probably his intent, as he could have placed the easel opposite the jury. I had to pull my feet under my chair for him to walk behind the easel to the jury box.

No one could have proved it was intentional if he'd just happened to trip over my feet, but I was very careful that he didn't. After I'd heard what he said about me, I had second thoughts.

He described an idyllic setting of peace and calm at this lovely little, historical church, using a soft, soothing voice I'd never heard him use before—until—*until* he changed his mask and went after me personally. Then his voice was louder and firm, and his previously benign expression was replaced with one of outrage, his eyes narrowing.

"First of all, Ms. Random knows a lot about the law. She's been a practicing paralegal off and on for several decades." Then he said in an even lower and sinister voice, "She has a professional working knowledge of the law, *and she knows how to sue folks.*" His disgust with that fact seemed a little out of place for an attorney who makes his living doing that exact thing. Then he addressed the hot tub with yet another new, manufactured scenario. He said, "This is what I believe the evidence will show. Ms. Random invited Fr. Martin to her house for dinner. He accepts, brings two of his Ukrainian students. After dinner, Ms. Random leaves for a few moments, reemerges without her blouse, much to the surprise of Fr. Martin and his students. Random asks the three men to join her in the hot tub. The three men feel uncomfortable, decline to join her, and leave." While Swartz was describing his imaginary scene with feigned shock at my supposed, shameless, clothing removal, I looked sideways at Martin. He was frowning and watching Swartz with an expression of complete innocence and intense curiosity as though he were hearing it for the first time. His face showed not the slightest betrayal of a conscience.

As Swartz continued his fanciful description, the commercial artist part of my brain awakened, and I visualized the scene he had created of the four of us in my hot tub. Only, my version was different, more like the childhood rhyme: "Rub a dub dub, three men in a tub." But, it wasn't the butcher, the baker and the candlestick maker. In my version, three men were sitting bolt upright and unsmiling in a hot tub with the water almost up to their shoulders, each of them fully clothed. The priest wore a black robe that accented the pristine whiteness of his clerical collar, and the two helmeted soldiers wore Czar Nicholas era, full-dress Russian uniforms—and heavy mustaches. There was not a woman in sight, much less one wearing only a bra and skirt. The image vanished when Swartz delivered his closing line, "I think this is a case about revenge. Thank you."

When the stage was cleared of Swartz's props, the next of the other two defense attorneys, Mr. Levangie for Fr. Martin, rose to give his performance in which I was portrayed as a villainess and Martin as a potential candidate for sainthood. The *Herald* reported that Levangie claimed, "The priest was merely trying to put rampant rumors among church members to rest when he told them what Random was doing…witnesses will testify that the statements attributed to Martin were not spoken by him."

Mr. Lauria followed on behalf of the Diocese of El Camino Real. It was claimed that I wasn't even a *real* Episcopalian with the implication that I was an interloper or heathen intruder who deserved everything the Episcopal Church chose to do to me because I wasn't *really* one of them.

At 10:35 AM., after a break, I was sworn and "testified on her own behalf."

I had tried many times to imagine what it would be like the moment I heard my name called by the clerk, and I would have to stand and walk to the witness stand. I'd always experienced nervousness just having to give a report in a meeting of people I knew, and I was the one who determined what I would say. Here, I had no sure idea of what might be asked, or what I would answer, before dozens of strangers. When I had to stand, would I feel as though I were about to collapse, the way I had while walking back to my pew after Fr. Martin denied me Communion? Would my hand shake as I raised it to take the oath? If it did, would people notice? Just the thought was making me stressed, and I tried to remember how a friend had taught me to breathe so as to relieve it.

It did no good as I nervously waited for the clerk to call my name. I reminded myself that this was the moment I had waited more than four years for—to publicly speak the truth—but it was also a moment that I dreaded. The room was mostly filled with Martin supporters whose faces made every effort to show me contempt, and Judge Dauphine had clearly shown her bias against us. I'd witnessed female judges treat women plaintiffs, defendants, and witnesses with disdain and intimidating exasperation. She could do it to me, and I would have no recourse.

To my left sat six people who wanted me to lose, with more seated behind us. Neil and I were the only two people present, other than a few friends, who wanted me to win. The truth and Neil were all I had. Suddenly, I heard my name called, and in an instant all my fears left me. I had the strength and courage that I'd prayed for as I rose from my chair, calmly walked to stand opposite the court clerk, and raised my right hand to take the oath.

Neil was my first questioner in direct examination. We went through the *real* hot tub incident, and the fact that on the night that I supposedly invited two Ukrainian soldiers and Fr. Martin into my hot tub while wearing only a bra and skirt, I had overnight guests, and Fr. Martin and his students—Ukrainian officers—had left the party at the same time as the other guests, except for Monica and John who were staying over.

I felt at ease on the stand, and remembered to look at the jurors while I simply told them the truth of what had happened. Responding to Neil's questions, I related my past in Palo Alto, told about my husband, my marriage, and how I'd always valued and protected my reputation while growing up. I said that in high school and college I got dumped many times by the young men I dated because I refused to do what some of the other girls did. I wasn't allowed to testify about anything that happened to me in church. Not the denial of Communion, the police charging me with criminal trespass, or any of the things pertaining to my being denied entry. I was allowed to testify about how Fr. Martin's slander and the treatment I got from others affected me. But, because I had refused to seek psychiatric help, the defense would later assert that I had suffered no mental or emotional harm.

Neil's questioning ended at the noon recess, and I went home to take care of my dogs, as I did each day of the trial. Betty Meyer came with me and we had lunch together while she nervously kept looking at her watch to make certain that I wouldn't be late.

After the lunch recess, I was back on the stand for cross-examination. Mr. Swartz went first. He asked me to go to a large blackboard and write each of the things I claimed Fr. Martin had said about me. Then he told me to write the names of each person who heard those things under each statement. It was a little difficult while standing at a blackboard in front of the whole courtroom to remember exactly who heard which of the various things and how many of them, but I did my best. I think Swartz's point was to make the jury believe from the beginning that only a few church people ever heard what Martin said about me. But, there were more than sixty whose actual names I finally learned, and only a few of them attended St. John's. There's no way of knowing how many others throughout the Monterey Peninsula heard it from those sixty.

During my testimony, the questions the defense attorneys asked in open court were nothing like the slimy, repetitious, personal ones they'd asked with no jury and spectators to observe them. They also had to be careful that they weren't too aggressive toward me, or badgered me, because the jury wouldn't like it. At one stage of his questioning, Swartz was approaching that danger, but backed down.

Mr. Lauria's questions were very often impossible to understand or even guess what he was trying to get at, although he'd clarified them a little from when he deposed me. At that time, his questions were such long, convoluted ramblings that even the other attorneys had to sometimes ask for explanations, and those explanations were almost as bad as the original questions.

He also constantly explained to everyone, over and over, the meaning of the question, "Does that *refresh* your memory?" At first it was amusing to watch his very serious explanation of what he described as a "legal term," but it got very annoying after constant repetition. For example, he explained it to Howard Sitton by saying, "What that is, sir, it is a term of art in the law that suddenly you read this document, and remember something by reading this you didn't recall before. That's what's meant by *refresh your memory*." It was insulting to the people testifying, as though they couldn't comprehend its obvious meaning. I found it strange that he had so much trouble explaining his own questions, but always insisted on explaining that one. Maybe that's the only one he, himself, could understand.

When the defense attorneys finished their questioning, Neil again questioned me on redirect, to clarify or elaborate on things the others had asked me. The jury was excused until the next morning, and no further conferences between the attorneys and Judge Dauphine followed their dismissal.

I went home and hugged my dogs. I was glad that my testimony was over. I thought I had done well, and I tried not to second-guess myself.

# CHAPTER FIFTEEN

# Thou Shalt Not Bear False Witness

On day number four, the Thursday morning Monterey *Herald* headline read: "Priest kept rumors flowing, parishioner says." The headline was front page all the way across and there were two small photos—one of Martin and one of me—which had been taken by the *Herald* photographer inside the courtroom. The article related the opening statements and my testimony.

The day began with the usual attorney conferences with the judge in chambers and out of the presence of the jury and the court reporter. At 9:07 AM. the jury was brought in and the court record states, "The court admonishes the audience regarding calling attorneys, witnesses, or parties, talking about the case on court premises, and closing the court when seating is filled.

"William Martin is sworn and testifies on behalf of plaintiff (we had summoned him) pursuant to Evidence Code section 776." Although Martin may have wanted to avoid testifying, he couldn't because this was a civil case, and the Fifth Amendment right regarding self-incrimination did not apply. For example, O.J. Simpson refused to testify in his criminal trial, but could not refuse in his civil trial.

Early on, Shapiro attempted to establish who hired Fr. Martin and what authority the Diocese of El Camino Real had over him. Shapiro asked, "And is it your understanding that your hiring by the Wardens and Vestrymen of St. John's Chapel had to be approved by the Diocese of El Camino Real?"

Martin answered, "Yes," and agreed that it was his understanding that the diocese (in the person of the bishop) also had the power and the authority to tell St. John's to terminate his position.

Lauria, the diocese attorney yelled, "Objection. Lacks foundation," and Dauphine sustained the objection. Shapiro then laid the foundation by asking Martin if he was "generally familiar with the canons of the Episcopal Church?" When Martin said he was, Shapiro directed his attention to Exhibit 61 regarding "Ecclesiastical Discipline," as stated in the Episcopal Church Canons.

Then, it was LeVangie who immediately objected on the grounds of relevance, and was joined by Lauria. Shapiro clarified, "The relevance, your Honor, concerns the ability of the diocese to discipline and take other action in the event of misconduct."

LeVangie added, "Also lacks foundation," and Dauphine said, "I think you need to lay a foundation through this witness before you ask him to read Exhibit 61."

Shapiro protested, "I asked him if he was familiar with it and recognizes it. He says he is familiar with it."

Judge Dauphine immediately ended Shapiro's questioning by saying, "*That's the end of that subject matter then. That* question and answer will be allowed. Next question."

I couldn't believe it. I'd heard Shapiro lay the foundation and establish the relevance and yet, *she'd stopped Martin's testimony cold.* Every time Shapiro had gotten close to *anything* regarding the Diocese's (bishop's) authority over Fr. Martin—to discipline, or even dismiss him—one or more of the defense attorneys jumped up to object. Their objections were almost always met with "Sustained." *In spite of her assurance of a fair trial, Dauphine continued to keep evidence out and cut off testimony that was harmful to the diocese and bishops—testimony that we had a right to present to the jury.* Those rulings were the proverbial writing on the wall of what was to come later, and it would be stunning.

The Canon Laws of the Episcopal Church USA are published on their official web site. There is nothing secret or confidential about them, and anyone can read for themselves that bishops have the authority to discipline or dismiss priests. Any person who is familiar with them, as William Martin said he was, could testify in court about them, and Martin had just said that he was knowledgeable. Shapiro had laid the foundation and the relevancy was that *the diocese's failure to discipline or dismiss Martin was what had brought us all into that courtroom.* There was too much evidence against Martin to keep it all out, but keeping out the evidence that the diocese had the authority to stop him and didn't, made the diocese appear to be helpless, and therefore harmless, meaning they could not be legally held to have had any responsibility for what Martin had done. No one will ever convince me that what Judge Dauphine did was *"inadvertent judicial error."* I will always believe that she knew exactly what she was doing, and that she did it with intent.

The rest of Martin's testimony was a series of answers that didn't match the things he had said in his deposition. Almost everything was a different version of what he had previously asserted as facts, and he was not doing well. LeVangie and Swartz were like a tag team taking turns jumping up to object, over and over, so as to keep Martin from saying even more that was so damaging. They knew what he was saying would all be refuted by our witnesses because they'd heard them in earlier depositions. They were so intent on keeping things out that at one point, LeVangie even tried to stop Shapiro from reading a portion of Martin's deposition. Surprisingly, Dauphine overruled his objection. Every time she made a ruling in our favor, my heart jumped in the hope that I was at last getting the fair trial I'd been promised, but the feeling never lasted. Shapiro had to argue to get even the simplest answers completed by Martin. The whole questioning seemed like just another exercise in futility. It appeared so blatant to me, that I thought the jury must surely be picking up on it.

Of all Martin's answers, the most revealing was his response to Shapiro's simple question, "What is the Vestry?" The question was so simple, that there was not a single objection from the defense. But it was poetic justice—there having been no other kind thus far. Martin replied, "The Vestry is the governing board of a parish church comprised of laymen, and a layman is someone who is not a priest." Then, without prompting, and against every attorney's admonishment to every witness (just answer the questions, and then stop talking) he leaned forward a little as he looked directly at the jurors and said to them, "So, you're all laymen. *I'm a priest.*" He may not have given any useful testimony for us, but those comments spoke a great deal about him, and judging from the jurors' expressions, they did not miss it.

Shapiro ended his examination by asking Martin, "Did you ever tell (naming each of our witnesses) that Rayn Random (stalked him, tried to lure him, and so forth) listing each statement separately with the name of each witnesses. Every time, Martin answered, "No."

Shapiro continued, "Did you ever tell Walter Alsky that Rayn Random had photographs of you all over her house? Did you ever tell Kim Rennick that Rayn Random was harassing you with so many phone calls you had to change your phone number? Did you ever tell Kim Rennick, 'Don't tell Rayn Random' my new phone number?" To every question, Martin answered, "No."

And then, Shapiro got in the question that had seemed impossible because of Judge Dauphine's earlier evidence ruling. He asked Martin: "Did you have any role in the decision to call the police when Rayn Random attempted to attend church in October of 2005?"

Martin answered, "I think that Howard Sitton had said to me that he was going to do that. But that would have been a vestry decision, and not mine." Neil asked if he'd approved of the decision and Martin replied, "At the time, yes."

When Dauphine asked if any of the defense attorneys wanted to cross-examine Martin, the response was a unanimous, "No questions, Your Honor." Dauphine's rulings had been very kind to them and their talkative client. There was no point in messing up a good thing by having Martin remain on the stand and say something unexpected, or open a door that would give Shapiro the right to question him again. If that happened, it would be harder for them to stop it. Prudence demanded that they get him off the stand as quickly as possible.

Our next witness was Jo Howard, scheduled for 10:30, right after the morning break, but Judge Dauphine had kept out so much testimony that Shapiro's questioning of Martin ended ahead of the anticipated time. It was barely past 10:00. Witnesses were not allowed in the courtroom until after they'd testified, so Jo had not yet arrived. No one can predict how long questioning will last, and sometimes it goes days over or under schedule.

Because of this supposedly inexcusable and unheard of lapse in witness scheduling by Shapiro, Judge Dauphine was fretting and complaining like a teenager who'd just been grounded. I'm quite sure she would have explained it away if it had been Andy Swartz, known to be a favorite of hers. She finally stopped and called the morning recess at 10:05.

Neil tried phoning Jo while I ran downstairs to watch for her. She had arrived in Monterey earlier in the week, but I hadn't seen nor spoken to her. When I saw her drive into the parking lot with her husband, Dale, I waved them over. Jo jumped out of the car, and she and I hurried up to the courtroom while Dale parked the car.

This was the fourth day of trial, and absolutely nothing had been going our way. At the end of each day Neil was certain that we were losing, although he didn't say it to me at the time. Jo Howard was, at last, the turning point for us. She was the first of our many witnesses who would prove to the jury that the Reverend William Martin not only said the things I'd claimed he said, but that his denials made him a liar, over and over.

Jo is a very attractive woman in every way. She's gracious, competent and articulate, and has a lovely face and figure without any of the cosmetic surgery Martin claimed she'd had. She was wearing a white linen suit and, to me, she looked like an angel who was appearing just in the nick of time. To Martin, she must have looked like his worst nightmare, at least if he had allowed his conscience to remind him of the horrid and untrue things he'd said about her. I glanced over at Martin, wondering if his clerical collar was beginning to choke him. It should have been, but he still had the same puzzled, innocent look of curiosity he'd had before. While Shapiro ran through the usual preliminary questions, I thought of Martin's behavior with Jo on a Sunday morning after church in 2003. I was still attending St. John's, but Martin had removed me from everything. I was standing at the foot of the church steps looking back up at the open doors as people were leaving the service. Jo had just stepped out and was shaking Martin's hand when he leaned forward and kissed her on the cheek. Knowing what he had said about her, I thought to myself that Judas could not have done it better.

After the preliminaries, Shapiro asked, "Would you tell the jury whether or not William Martin ever mentioned to you Rayn Random's hot tub?" She said that he had and that it was in 2002. "He (Martin) said that—he called, said that—and I don't know if it was right after the event was supposed to have happened…he called and said that there had been a vestry meeting. The vestry meeting had been held at Rayn Random's home.[28] And that after the meeting ended and people left, that she got him aside, or he stayed there, and said that, 'Why don't we go into the hot tub together? You're frustrated, you're uptight. Do you want to go into the hot tub?'" When Shapiro asked her if she had believed that had actually occurred, she said, "I had no reason not to."

Shapiro: "Any particular reason you believed him?"

Ms. Howard: "He was the priest of the church." She said that he repeated the claim every few months when he would be ranting and talking. At one of those times he said, "Can you

---

28    Vestry meetings are always held at church.

believe that Rayn Random invited me into her hot tub?" Another time, he asked, "Can you believe Rayn Random invited me into her hot tub, and can you believe that I would do that?"

Shapiro asked Ms. Howard, "Would you tell the jury whether William Martin ever used the words 'restraining order' in connection with Rayn Random?" She said he had, and the first time was after a church service (2003) in his office. "He said that he had gotten a restraining order against Rayn Random to keep her away from him. He said that she was stalking him." Asked if she believed him, she said yes and the reason was, "Because he said that, I believed that she was stalking him. He was the rector, the priest, and I regarded him highly..." She testified that there were many times when William Martin used the words "stalking" and "restraining order" with respect to me, just as he had with the hot tub. She related one incident as follows:

"I can remember one—it was in the afternoon. I think it was a Saturday that I was at the church. And, I think I was setting up tables for a luncheon after church, and he came in and said, 'Rayn Random is here. I know she's here.' And I said, 'You know *what?*' He said, 'Rayn Random is here. She's out there someplace outside the church…would you go see where she is?'

"So, I mean it shocked me. And so, I looked, and I didn't see her car. I didn't see her anywhere. And I told him I didn't see her anywhere. I said, 'She's not out there.'"

When Shapiro asked about the next time, Ms. Howard said, "Again, it would come up every so often—any time there was a conversation—that he got going about Rayn, then he would say that again." She explained that Martin had said it at her home and at his home.

Shapiro changed the questioning to Scott Jackson, and Ms. Howard said that she was acquainted with him and, "Scott Jackson was a young naval officer stationed at the postgraduate school."

Shapiro asked, "Would you tell the jury whether or not

William Martin ever made a statement about Rayn Random to Scott Jackson in your presence?" Ms. Howard related the times and various places—her home, Fr. Martin's home and restaurants. She also testified that she and Dale socialized with Scott and his fiancé. The Defense objected at every opportunity—they probably knew what was coming—and Shapiro was finally able to get to the question he wanted to ask.

Shapiro: "As best you can recall, what did William Martin say about Rayn Random to Scott Jackson in your presence?"

Ms. Howard: "First this was, of course, after he was not associating with Rayn Random. And Scott Jackson was engaged and the wedding was going to be held in Texas, and on Scott's list were ourselves, Rayn Random, and I think probably William Martin was to be a part of the service." She then repeated the statement he made, "'Scott, you cannot invite Rayn Random. She cannot be at the wedding. She cannot be there because she is a problem. She's stalking me, and I cannot possibly be there and be a part of it if Rayn Random is there.' He simply said that she was stalking him, she was a problem and wouldn't go away, and he could not be there. He could not go to the wedding."

Shapiro asked, "Did you attend Scott Jackson's wedding," and Ms. Howard answered yes. "Did Rayn Random attend?" Ms. Howard said, "No. She did not."

Listening to Jo's testimony, I began to feel better than I had in over four years because at last, the first rays of truth had finally broken through the dark clouds that had surrounded and followed me everywhere. And the truth was coming from someone other than me.

Shapiro asked Ms. Howard, "Do you recall whether or not William Martin used the word 'stalking' with respect to Rayn Random on any other occasion?" She answered that he continued to do so in early 2004. She said, "Same thing, that Rayn Random was stalking him, that he...that she was not quitting. She was calling him."

Ms. Howard related yet another incident: "It might have been July, August of 2003. Well, this particular time, he was in London. And, I, of course, was in Monterey. He was very upset on the other end of the phone. He said that he had been sick, but that he had called the house and there were these lurid messages from Rayn Random on his telephone…He said that Rayn Random had called and left a message for him to come for Champagne."

Shapiro asked, "Did William Martin ever make statements to you about Rayn Random's anatomy?" Ms. Howard said that he had, "The first time I recall, probably 2002, I was again at the church setting up for some event. Rayn had come into the Fellowship Hall and she was arranging flowers for the altar. She…I remember it so vividly…because it was so unlike her. She had blue jeans and a blue sweater on that was fitted. It was not overly tight, but it was fitted. And her breasts showed. I mean, you know, you could see that her breasts didn't show, but the profile was there. And she was over in the kitchen area doing the flowers for the altar. And she had backed up and was standing against the far wall. And he came over and said to me, 'Look at that. Look at that. Look at her. She has—she has—look at her breasts. You know they're blowups.'

"And I mean that's a shock to me. I mean it was a shock to me. But…I looked and that's why I remember Rayn so vividly. And he said. 'She, you know, those are blowups, and those breasts aren't real. I think she's a man.'"

Ms. Howard's testimony from the witness stand was the first account I'd actually heard of the full story. We hadn't taken her pre-trial deposition because by then, she and Dale had moved from Monterey. I, too, remembered that day because of her description of my clothes—I don't think I'd ever worn jeans to church any other time—and Martin, Jo, Dale and I had a brief, friendly conversation in the kitchen after I'd finished arranging the flowers. Martin and I were still friends at the time—at least I thought we were—and I never suspected, nor could I have believed that my "friend," the priest of my church, was even then saying such bizarre things about me.

When Shapiro asked if Martin had made reference to my anatomy or my gender on any other occasion, Ms. Howard answered, "Yes, I would say several more times in 2002 and certainly in 2003. Wherever we might be together. I mean, if we were at dinner, somehow the conversations always ended up before the evening was over about Rayn Random."

Shapiro: "And was that because someone else brought up her name or because William Martin brought up her name?"

Ms. Howard looked straight at Shapiro and said, "No one else brought up her name."

"And when William Martin first made these statements about how her breasts must be fake and he thinks she's a man," Shapiro asked, "did you believe that he was truthful?" Ms. Howard explained, "You put...you put the idea into someone's head and you begin to wonder. I mean, you start observing and wondering. That's as much as I can tell you."

"When you first met Rayn Random, or first were aware of Rayn Random at St. John's, how did other people relate to her?" Ms. Howard answered, "Well, Rayn was a very quiet lady. We would sit up, halfway up in the church pews. And I would—I noticed as I began to be at church that she sat to the back. And she would simply sit at the service, as far as I knew, and I would notice her when she would go up to Communion. And, she would always speak to people. She was quiet. And people spoke back to her. She talked with people that were maybe...they were on the Altar Guild...they were friendly."

Shapiro: "Did that ever change?"

Ms. Howard: "In my own words, I think some people began to treat her like she had the plague. People didn't talk to her as much. She would come in to the Fellowship Hall and people just turned or went their, you know, went their way or had their coffee. I remember thinking one time I didn't... I didn't know how she was doing that (putting up with their behavior)… I remember that."

Shapiro asked her to describe what happened in 2003 when I walked into Episcopal Church Women meetings. Ms. Howard told him, "I had started attending the meetings, and Rayn walked in. There were two or three occasions. The meetings were held once a month. And we would be talking and there would be things going on. People were serving lunch. And you know, the normal talking, so forth. And suddenly, when Rayn would come in, it would be dead silence. It would just get very quiet. And I don't remember anybody greeting her."

Shapiro asked if she could tell the court when was the last time she had heard any of the statements that he'd asked her about, repeated in the community, Ms. Howard answered, "Two nights ago…I'm just here on a week's visit, and I was with a gathering on Tuesday evening. And of course the conversation comes around to this because it—obviously, people know about it. And, this lady…some of them started talking and I did not…"

That was as far as her reply went because suddenly objections started flying like a flock of startled birds. Shapiro attempted another approach, and objections took off again. It resulted in a side bar conference that was off the record. Jo Howard was cut off and not allowed to disclose what was said about me that evening, but the implication was that it was nothing good.

When things settled down again, Shapiro asked: "Did there ever come a time when you began to disbelieve the truth of the statements we've been discussing here today?"

Ms. Howard: "Yes. Because he—William Martin—was saying things and making derogatory statements about other people."

LeVangie shouted, "Objection, your Honor. Move to strike, relevance, 352," but the court overruled the objection.

Shapiro finished with, "Thank you. I have nothing further."

Martin's attorney, LeVangie, had questions. He inquired,

"Ms. Howard, while you still lived on the Monterey Peninsula did you personally ever treat Rayn Random inappropriately because you believed some of these statements?" LeVangie apparently expected her to say she did not—most people would probably be too embarrassed to admit such a thing— but Jo speaks the truth…"I avoided her." Asked how many times, she said, "I was going to St. John's every Sunday. I was involved in other things in the church. William Martin asked me not to have anything to do with Rayn Random, and I did not."

Swartz also had questions. "My question is are you aware, about two months before you moved back east, that Ms. Random was asked to sever her connection and pray elsewhere?" She answered, "Yes, I had heard that…I knew that he had tried to remove her from the church." Pressing on, Swartz inquired, "Okay. And you thought that was a good idea, didn't you, at that time?" When she answered, "No," I don't think Swartz got the answer he expected.

He continued his pursuit, "Okay. So, on the one hand, you're telling us you believed what Fr. Martin was saying, that this woman had been stalking him and harassing him, but on the other hand, you're saying that you don't believe it would be appropriate to ask her to stay away from the church, is that correct?" Ms. Howard said, "He's a priest. The church is there to give comfort to people. If there were problems, then they should have been resolved."

Switching to his slow, condescending voice that Swartz used with women who didn't oblige him with the answers he wanted, he said, "We all agree with that proposition ma'am. But, Fr. Martin, you testified moments ago, was afraid of Rayn Random, correct?" Ms. Howard clarified for him. "He *said* he was afraid of Rayn Random."

Swartz was not getting Ms. Howard where he wanted her to go, and his frustration was becoming apparent. "And, you believed that he was afraid of her, didn't you?" Swartz spoke the words, "didn't you," reminiscent of a Perry Mason moment, not as a question, but as an in-your-face demand that she *confess.*

Ms. Howard calmly answered, "In the beginning I did." Swartz zeroed in hoping for a verbal victory, "And, he asked you to go outside to see if she was outside so he did not have to be near her, correct?" Again, the word *correct* was a demand.

Without losing a smidge of composure, Ms. Howard said, "Yes, but he was acting foolish." Finally Swartz demanded in a loud voice, "Well, he was *scared to death of her, wasn't he?*" Ms Howard, still completely unflustered, said, "No."

Swartz had to back off, so he switched to the hot tub. After several preliminary questions, asked: "Do you feel that it would be inappropriate for Ms. Random to offer the use of her hot tub to the rector of your church, whoever it may be?" When she replied that she did not feel it would be inappropriate, Swartz appeared to be shocked—or at least, pretended to be—and said, "You would think that would be okay? Would that be alright?" Ms. Howard replied, "I think so."

Then Swartz misquoted the previous testimony saying, "Okay. So, if Fr. Martin said that Rayn Random asked him into her hot tub..." He had quickly changed the description from *offered the use of* to *asked him into*—"you didn't see anything inappropriate about that, is that correct?"

She answered, "Except for the way he made it sound." Swartz inquired if she meant the tone of his voice and she said, "Lure. Lured." Switching into a doubting, skeptical sounding voice he asked, "You're sure that's not your imagination?"

Ms. Howard firmly said, "It's in the testimony. I don't have that kind of imagination. No. He said *lure.*"

Changing topics, Swartz suggested that there was a lot of gossip going on at St. John's... "correct?"

Ms. Howard surprised him again when she said, "You know, I don't agree with you. I don't think that's true. The people at St. John's are perhaps more of a senior group. And they come to church, they go to Fellowship Hall, they have coffee, they take some cookies home and that's it. It's—it's not a real social church."

Swartz asked if she was "telling the ladies and gentlemen of the jury under oath that Fr. Martin was the only one that gossiped?" Ms. Howard said that Fr.Martin "certainly was the leader."

Trying again, Swartz asked, "So you never heard any gossip from anyone during your three or four years at St. John's other than Fr. Martin?"

Ms. Howard smiled and said, "You're absolutely right."

That was the end for Swartz.

Jo had been a wonderful witness and just what we needed to finally stop the tide that kept pushing against us. I wanted to jump up and hug her as she walked past me on her way out of the courtroom, but we didn't look at each other. She had told the truth. Not one person could refute it, and Swartz and LeVangie had lost that round. But the biggest loser was Father William Martin.

# CHAPTER SIXTEEN

# And Each in Turn

Our next witness, Walter Alsky, has thick gray hair, a smile that lights up his face, and a suggestion of playfulness about him. After he took the oath and was seated in the witness box, Shapiro asked him the usual introductory questions about himself. When he asked, "How old are you," Walter replied, "Oh, on June 30th of this year, I have the pleasure of saying I will be 90." He was so engaging from the very beginning that it was impossible for anyone not to like him except, of course, the teeth-clenched people to my left and behind me.

When Shapiro asked if he'd ever heard "William Martin say things about Rayn Random," Walter said that he had, and as he began to state them there were all kinds of objections when he couldn't remember exact dates. Finally he said, "All I can say is I'm not good at times. I didn't keep a diary. If I had known, I should have, but it was before I met Ms. Random." After more objections, he said, "More than a year ago, let me put it that way. I remember my divorce date, I remember my father's dying, but these little incidentals, I don't have, you know..."

There were more objections until he said it was sometime in 2004. Dauphine overruled the objections, and Shapiro asked the question again. LeVangie had to give it one more try and called out, "Objection. Vague as to time." It was ignored.

Walter continued, "Well, I heard about the restraining order, and I heard that she was harassing him, phoning him. Fr. Martin told me that she had pictures of him on every wall in her house. And the first time I entered her home I said, 'Oh, you took all your pictures down,' and she didn't know what I was talking about."

He also confirmed that he had believed the statements about me and described the first time we met at Quail Lodge, "Well, once a month they have an orchestra and…the public are invited to dance. And we (he, Clifford, and other friends) were there. We used to go quite often. And Ms. Random arrived with a party (Carole) that we all knew. I didn't know who she was until somebody in our crowd said who she was."

Shapiro asked what was Walter's reaction when he learned who I was, and he said, "I hate to…I thought what is that horrible, slutty woman doing here? Because I heard all this so-called—I will say garbage now—about her, and I just thought she was just despicable. I just could not believe she was there."

Shapiro asked him how I behaved that evening and Walter said, "Well, as I watched her, it was that she was reserved and she was sort of stand-offish, and she was like—she was afraid to enter—I would say maybe even uncomfortable that she was there. And you know, she was afraid of people…"

Walter was right about that. I hadn't wanted to be at Quail Lodge that night, but Carole had insisted that I couldn't keep hiding from the rest of the world, and I needed to get out of my house and face people because I had done nothing wrong. She told me that we were just going to join a group of friends. They were mostly her friends, people I didn't know at all except for Adrianne, who managed to keep her back turned to me and ignore me. She made it very clear that she wasn't pleased to see me, which didn't portend a happy evening. Because Carole and I had taken her car, I didn't have the option to immediately leave, which I would otherwise have done. Several tables had been pushed together to create one big one, so I picked a seat and resigned myself to being an unwelcome, non-participant. Walter and Clifford invited the other women to dance, and the two couples who were there danced with each other. Finally, thanks to Walter, the evening brightened a bit.

Shapiro asked him if he talked to me at the dance, and

Walter said, "Eventually I did. Just to be polite. And nothing was discussed about her problem or anything. It was just a friendly chit-chat of nonsense. And finally, I began to say to myself, this is not the woman I anticipated that she was. She was not any of those things that I had in my mind. It turned out to be, I thought, a lovely evening. And I'm glad that I met her. Let me put it that… they played a polka, and we danced the polka." Asked if we became friends, he said, "I think I'm a friend of hers."

Shapiro took Walter back to the two times that he and Clifford went to St. John's with me. "When you went to church with Rayn, did you have an understanding as to where she normally sat?" Walter said, "It's my understanding she sat in the front pew, based on what Fr. Martin told me." Asked where I did sit, Walter told Shapiro, "The third row from the back." Asked to describe what happened after the service, Walter related, "Well, Ms. Random said we might as well go to the community room for coffee. And as we approached the community room, they naturally slammed the door in our faces, and stood guard, and wouldn't let us in."

About the second trip to St. John's the following Sunday, he said, "The first thing that happened was that the assistant district attorney Stefanie Hulsey, and her husband tried to prevent us from going in. And finally we entered. I think church services were delayed about a half hour. I don't know why that was. But I had to laugh. They kept running up to the organ player, keep playing another song. Play another song." Asked what happened after the service, Walter answered, "We were greeted by two charming police officers. Well, they interviewed…took whatever we wanted to say, and they said we were accused of trespassing."

LeVangie yelled another objection that it was hearsay, and Dauphine sustained it.

Shapiro had no further questions. Swartz took over on cross examination. He said to Walter, "You've described a number of incidents earlier and my first question is did Ms. Random ever tell you that she was upset about anything that Reverend Martin or St. John's had done?" Walter told him, "I would say she was upset, very, and it seems that it was under her impression that when... Fr. Martin signed the document, that he did not tell the truth. Her attorney said she was free to go to church."

LeVangie objected again, "Move to strike as hearsay."

Swartz then said, "Your Honor, my question was, did Ms. Random ever tell you she was upset about anything."

Walter immediately said, "Of course."

And then Judge Dauphine interrupted, "Just a minute. I need to rule on the motion. The motion is granted. The reference to the statement by the attorney, or what she said her attorney said, is stricken. You are to disregard it, as difficult as that may be."

The cross examination of Walter was not going smoothly for the defense attorneys. Walter was obviously a very straightforward person. Swartz quoted Walter as having said in his prior deposition, "To tell you the truth, at the time it wasn't that important. It was just gossip in a way."

Swartz quickly moved to reinforce that Walter had called it "gossip." He said, "And those were your words when you were asked questions about a year ago. Correct?"

Testimony hit another bump when Walter began to answer, but got only as far as, "A...," when Dauphine jumped in with, "The question, sir, is whether...," and then Walter interrupted *her* by saying, "Yes, I know. " Judge Dauphine finally finished her sentence saying, "Whether those were your words at the time your deposition was taken."

Walter finally got to make his point, "If I had said it was just gossip, I didn't put any—I believed what was said, but...it wasn't true is what I'm getting at. But at the beginning I thought it was true. So when I used the word—I'm not that brilliant. I'm not an attorney. I might have said it was just gossip. But I could also have said it was hearsay or it was just whatever." There was a slight murmur of amusement from the gallery.

After a lunch recess, Walter returned to testify further. Lauria, representing the Diocese, did just as the others had. He tried to pass off the things Martin said simply as gossip, not anything as consequential as defamation. He asked, "Is it true Mr. Alsky, that when you heard these things, that you just didn't consider it to be all that important?" Walter said, "I just thought...I thought it was something terrible that was being said about an awful woman...she was not.....a very good word."

Mr. Lauria kept pressuring him to say it wasn't important and only gossip, and there were various interruptions by attorneys and the judge, until Walter finally decided to give his definition of the word "gossip," and this time Walter didn't stop until he'd said exactly what he wanted to say, without being interrupted by anyone.

"And my definition of gossip, when I say gossip, is somebody out defaming somebody, telling awful, awful stories and untruths, now that's my definition of gossip."

It continued back and forth with Lauria attempting to trivialize what Martin had said and that no one really paid any attention, but it didn't work with Walter. Lauria finally said, "Thank you, Mr. Alsky."

None of the other attorneys had further questions. When Judge Dauphine said, "Thank you very much, sir," Walter turned to her and answered teasingly, "I don't want to go." Everyone laughed. They'd been enjoying his testimony except, of course, the gallery sitting just behind me. Judge Dauphine said, "I'm glad your nerves have been calmed."

Walter asked, "May I come back?" Judge Dauphine told him, "The courtroom door is open." Everyone smiled at Walter when he left, clearly appreciating his folksy honesty.

Our next witness was Dr. John Steel, an oral and maxillofacial surgeon, and the husband of Anita Steel. He had also been a member of St. John's for more than thirty years and had served in almost every church capacity except priest. He had been chairman of the search committee that interviewed candidates to be the rector of St. John's, and ultimately hired William Martin.

Shapiro asked him about Martin, and Dr. Steel said, "I've socialized with him at restaurants, at our home, at the rectory, his home, and church functions, as well as other private homes."

"The statements made to me by Fr. Martin were that Rayn Random was stalking him, harassing him, that she was making numerous phone calls, that he had to change his telephone number, and that he needed to obtain a restraining order against her...These remarks were made on church property, or phone calls, or at his home, or at our home."

Shapiro inquired if he treated me any differently after he'd read Exhibit 1, and Dr. Steel replied, "The answer would be yes. It's more of how I thought of her. Prior to this, and during 2003 and 2004, I believed Fr. Martin. I supported that she was possibly committing all of these issues. And then after March, I realized that I was wrong, and that I had a different perspective of Rayn Random. I really even still to this day don't know her well."

After Dr. Steel, our next witness was Kim Rennick, and Shapiro asked her about a phone call she'd received from Fr. Martin in 2004. Kim related what Fr. Martin told her. "That he had a stalker and he was giving me this phone number, and that I was not to under any circumstances, give it out to anyone else. I was duty bound because he was in a great deal of emotional trauma because he was being stalked by this lady. And I asked who it was. He said, 'Oh, you know...the one that used to be a man what is really, you know, all gussied up all the time with the hats.' And I said, well, I don't know who you're talking about. And he told me Rayn Random. I didn't know Rayn Random's full name. I just knew the name Rayn."

Exhibit 31 was produced, a copy of Kim's personal phone directory and the page on which she had written Martin's instructions not to give out the number and why, with my name. Shapiro asked Kim, "Do you remember anything else William

Martin said about Rayn Random on that occasion, about her personally, or her gender or her anything?"

She answered, "Well, he—yeah. He said that he wanted her out of the church and he wanted her gone. She was causing a problem. That she was disturbing to the parishioners, which confused me, because I wasn't disturbed by her. And that he doubted that she was really a female and a few other things like that."

Under cross examination, Mr. Swartz asked, "And you knew Rayn Random was a woman. You knew that, correct?" Kim said that she assumed I was a woman. "She presented herself as a woman. I accepted that. I accept people pretty much at face value."

"And now," said Swartz. "I want to put into context Fr. Martin's remarks. He (Martin) said, 'Well, no woman of that age would have great looking legs like hers.' So in a sense, it was a compliment, wasn't it ma'am?" Kim would have none of it and told Swartz, "No. It was a derogatory compliment."

Swartz later asked questions about why she, Kim, had left St. John's and he became frustrated when she refused to let him put words into her mouth and agree with him. He turned to Judge Dauphine and said, "Objection, Your Honor. There is no question. *The woman* is just speaking. And I will move to strike the reason she left the church in 2004."

Dauphine said, "The court will strike that portion of the witness' response. However, the court requests, Mr. Swartz, that you refer to her as a witness or by her name, rather than, 'the woman.'"

It was a public reprimand that I appreciated and enjoyed immensely because of his condescending attitude toward women. Swartz said, "Thank you Your Honor. I apologize." Kim added, "That's a subtle little thing there."

Pamela Norton took the stand next, but had nothing of any particular interest or substance to say other than what she'd given earlier in her deposition answers.

At 4:13, jurors were excused until Friday, and Dauphine and the attorneys met in her chambers. It was the end of day four.

The next day, Friday, everyone but the jury was present while there were more discussions between counsel and the judge, and Mr. Swartz requested that the court continue to admonish the jurors regarding media. By 9:00 a.m. Juror #11 had not yet arrived. We still had one alternate juror, the other having replaced the woman who asked to be excused for fear of retribution from her Episcopal church. The waiting, with the entire courtroom focused on the empty chair in the jury box, lasted only six minutes, but it seemed like half an hour, and I couldn't help but imagine what a delay would mean if she were ill or had an emergency. Everyone was relieved when Juror #11 took her place.

The headline in the Monterey *Herald* that day was, "Priest denies allegations. Says he signed agreement to stop gossip." There was a quote in bold type from Walter's testimony, "I thought everybody was welcome in church and there's no such thing as trespassing." The story continued:

"The witnesses said they initially believed Martin and shunned Random because Martin was the pastor of their parish, St. John's Episcopal Church in Monterey. When they realized that Martin was also making derogatory comments about others in the parish, they said they changed their minds and eventually shared with Random the things Martin said about her.

"Martin took the stand and denied the allegations. When he signed a settlement agreement with Random in 2005, admitting he'd made the defamatory and false statements, he said, he did so only to end a period of destructive gossip, but was not being truthful. 'I wanted a release from a situation that had become a burden, a distraction from collective life together and had caused pain,' he said, adding that he 'did not want to go into a lawsuit with Random.'" The article also stated that, "All of the witnesses, including Martin, said Random had never been disruptive on the church grounds or in the church services." I was very gratified that the *Herald* was being so objective in its reporting.

The first witness we called on Friday morning was Ms. Joan Fontaine, the famous actress who had twice been nominated for an Academy Award, and had won the Best Actress Oscar for her performance in Alfred Hitchcock's film, *Suspicion*. She had lived on the Monterey coast for 24 years, had been married in St. John's Chapel, and was a longtime parishioner, although I don't remember ever seeing her attend.

Shapiro went through the usual opening questions in which he almost sounded like the straight man for her English humor. When he asked if she was employed—she'd recently turned 90—she said, "No," without elaboration. He asked if she was retired and she answered, "Retired indeed." When he inquired, "And what did you do before you retired," people were already smiling. While Ms. Fontaine maintained a perfectly serious expression, she matter-of-factly replied, "Wrote a book, did some speaking engagements, and got the Oscar." The bit of appreciative laughter that followed was a very welcome, light-hearted way to begin another day of testimony. Many in the courtroom had grown up watching Joan Fontaine movies, and it isn't every morning that one gets to meet an academy award-winning actress. Her beauty was still incandescent, and when she spoke her voice was as wonderful as it had always been.

We have a number of celebrities in Monterey and scores of others who are always visible around the Peninsula when they're performing here or playing golf. Ms. Fontaine and Clint Eastwood, also an Academy Award winner and once the mayor of Carmel, are the best known of our famous residents.[29]

Shapiro asked Ms. Fontaine, "Have you ever told Rayn

---

[29]     St. John's Chapel is not without its own glow of celebrity status, as Collis Huntington, President of Southern Pacific Company, and Charles Crocker, patriarch of the Crocker Banking family, had participated in the planning of the church which was built in the 1880s. Worshipers included President Theodore Roosevelt and dozens of notable guests from the elegant, nearby Del Monte Hotel, which is now the Naval Post Graduate School.

Random anything that William Martin told you?" She answered, "I've only spoken to her once, on the telephone. She had called me about an award of some sort, theatrical. And I said to her I was terribly sorry that there was this schism...I'm a protector of women. I feel that we were given a bad go at life. And I care terribly about honesty."

When Shapiro asked how she met Martin, she recalled, "Oh, I was at a dinner given by the organist from the church...his name is Clay Couri. And there was an empty place in front of me at the table. And then Fr. Martin came and took that place."

Although she remembered many instances when William Martin talked about me, and remembered the things he had told her, she was not able to place the dates, and the objections from the defense attorneys were constant. She did say that he had talked about me often: "I would say every time I was with him. When this—I don't know about the early days, but from then on, yes...I imagine we met three or four times a year." She wanted to testify to everything she'd heard Martin say, but couldn't because of all the objections over the time factor.

Judge Dauphine was not at all solicitous in helping her recall approximate times, as she had been with Walter. None of the defense attorneys had a single question for her, and I think they—and Judge Dauphine—wanted her off the stand as quickly as possible because the jury was so attentive to every word she spoke, and her celebrity status could create headlines beyond Monterey. As she was leaving the stand, she said, "Hardly worth dressing." The jury heard her and chuckled as Clifford escorted her out of the courtroom. Judge Dauphine called after her, "You look beautiful. And I'm glad you were here."

Even though her testimony had been mostly suppressed, her mere appearance spoke volumes, and I was very touched that she had voluntarily stepped forward to support me. We had never met, at church or anywhere else. She didn't know me.

Our next witness was Anita Steel, Dr. Steel's wife. We

attended different services on Sundays, but I had seen her at church functions, and she and John had attended a Christmas party at my home. Anita served in the Sunday school, twice on the Vestry, organized special programs, and Martin once told me that she and John were the church's largest financial contributors.

After the preliminary questioning, she testified, "Fr. Martin told me that he was scared, he was being stalked and he needed to change his phone number, she was making inappropriate sexual advances, she had appeared under dressed at times. He said she would not leave him alone, and she was calling him night and day, and he wanted to get his phone number changed to avoid that. He told me that many times in 2004."

Shapiro asked her if Martin made his statements at vestry meetings. She said he had, including his claim, "she appeared once without a shirt on. He made (the statements) pretty much every vestry meeting that I was present."

She said that she knew about the document containing Martin's admissions from a vestry meeting. Swartz objected "to the extent she's getting into attorney/client communications." Dauphine obliged and ordered, "An objection will be sustained as to any attorney/client conversations. That means relating any information you may have learned from an attorney for the vestry."

Swartz's objections implied that he represented the vestry *and* William Martin during those meetings, but when I had asked him in an earlier letter to clarify his position, he never responded. Ms. Steel set the record straight by saying, "There was no attorney for the vestry present. Jim Cook was the vestry attorney, hired by Pam Norton and me. Andy Swartz appeared with Fr. Martin and said…" When she tried to continue, Swartz cut her off again, this time, with a hearsay objection, and Judge Dauphine sustained it. But, it wouldn't be very long before Ms. Steel's testimony would stop the objections—cold.

Shapiro continued, "During the vestry meeting, did William Martin make any statements about Exhibit 1 other than he signed it to get rid of Ms. Random?"

Ms. Steel answered, "Yes. He said in a loud voice, 'I'm the victim here. I should be protected. I—I didn't—I didn't—I didn't sign this—I didn't say these things. I just need to get rid of her. She's stalking me. And, I'm fearful.'"

Asked if she ever heard William Martin make any negative or derogatory statements about me after that, she said, "Yes. Any time she approached the church or it was perceived she was going to be coming to church. I was an 8:00 o'clocker, so I didn't come to the service Rayn came to. I would be leaving, and she would be coming. So I was listening to comments made after the 8:00 o'clock service as I was leaving, (they were) fearful that she might be coming to the next service. After the 8:00 o'clock service, Fr. Martin would be vocal about whether or not Rayn Random would show up, and he was looking for people to be watchful, and to let him know, and to be on guard, hoping to keep her out of the next service."

After LeVangie cross examined Ms. Steel, her most damning testimony was about to arrive. Shapiro, on re-direct said, "Mr. LeVangie asked you if you ever said William Martin was dangerous or whether you were afraid of him. Let me ask you, do you have any reason…to fear him?"

Ms. Steel said that she did, and Shapiro asked her to "tell us what it is."

LeVangie shouted his objection that it was irrelevant, and he was overruled. What came next was mind-blowing for many in that courtroom.

Ms. Steel said, "I no longer attend St. John's, and the reason I don't attend St. John's is because the last time I attended St. John's and went to the altar for Communion, Fr. Martin assaulted me with the (Communion) cup. When I reached to tip it to my lips, he shoved it against my face and sloshed it against my face and down my neck, cutting my lip. I haven't been back since, and I'll never go back."

There were no further questions—from anyone.

It took a lot of courage for most of our witnesses to speak the truth, risking a potential backlash from friends,[30] the church, their neighbors, their patients, and at times it almost brought me to tears of gratitude as I silently said, "Thank you."

Howard Sitton was the last witness we called that day. Shapiro asked him about the nature of his first conversation with me (prior to my excommunication).

Mr. Sitton made a telling slip of the tongue when he said, "I met her at a side door and asked that she leave…the priest *didn't* want to come out that door." His slip of the tongue told the truth—that Fr. Martin never used that door, and didn't really want to use it on that Sunday morning. Sitton then admitted that I wasn't blocking the door, prompting Shapiro to ask, "Why did you ask her to leave?"

Sitton with serious conviction replied, "We thought there might be a confrontation…I believe the priest thought so." Shapiro followed with, "And William Martin asked you to ask Rayn Random to leave simply so he wouldn't have to walk past her. Is that right?" Sitton answered, "Yes."

Shapiro asked him if he had wondered at the time, why William Martin had asked him to make Rayn Random leave. Mr. Sitton—ever unquestioning and eager to perform any task for William Martin—raised his chin and proudly answered, "No. I did not wonder." His attitude and the way he answered the question seemed to be right out of the Middle Ages. He'd sworn allegence to his liege lord, and his devotion was unquestioning.

Shapiro continued, "And the apparent desire to confront the priest on the church property was simply for failing to honor your suggestion, or insistence, that she leave, correct?" The answer was, "Yes." And when Shapiro inquired, "Did she do anything else to provoke a confrontation with William Martin?" Sitton said, "Not to my knowledge."

---

30    Attorney Andy Swartz and Dr. Steel were running partners.

Later, on the subject of the admission statement, Shapiro asked Mr. Sitton: "Did the possibility that the rector of St. John's Parish had made the seven statements set forth in Exhibit 1 concern the vestry?" Mr. Sitton said he was sure that it did, but no one asked Fr. Martin if he, in fact, said those things because, "I think they felt as I felt, that I simply couldn't believe some of those things." When Shapiro inquired if Sitton ever asked Martin, he said that he had, but Martin never told him.

Shapiro then asked if anyone ever sought to determine if Fr. Martin had gotten a restraining order against me, and Mr. Sitton told him, "No, we didn't, because we—it would have required an investigation which we wouldn't know how to mount. It would require money, and the church is in dire financial straights. And we had in our hands the evidence that someone wanted to confront the priest on the church grounds."

His excuses were inexcusable. The courthouse is two blocks from St. John's. It would have taken less than thirty minutes for someone, anyone, to *walk* to the courthouse, check the records and find out that there was no restraining order. There are computers he could have used, and a clerk would have gladly assisted him. Andy Swartz could have given them an instant answer. He knew in October 2005 that there was none *because he threatened me with one*, and even before that—as Martin's attorney—he would have been the person who prepared the petition for one. A phone call to the police department would have told them there was none. But most obviously, the Reverend William Martin could have simply opened his mouth and told the truth. All of those things would have cost them absolutely nothing.

As I listened to witness after witness I wondered, didn't some of these otherwise intelligent people—many of whom had college degrees, owned successful businesses, were professionals, and religious stalwarts of the church—ever go to bed at night questioning if they were doing the right thing? Wondering what if…? What if Martin's admission was true, and an innocent woman was being persecuted? At times, listening to it all, it made me wonder about the future of the Episcopal Church, and the Diocese of El Camino Real in particular. If the bishops who had lied, and the priests who had lied, and the elected church officers, who enabled and covered for them without questioning, were removed, what would be left of the Church? The answer is simple. What would remain is God, those parishioners who actually listen to His words, priests like Frs. Carl Hansen and Alan Wolter, and men like "Monsignor" Les Reed. *That* would be truly Biblical.

On re-cross examination, Shapiro asked about the Sunday that the police were called to St. John's. "Is it your testimony to this jury that you actually feared physical violence from this woman?" Sitton insisted, "I thought it could occur based on the wording in the letters."

Shapiro, in a disbelieving voice asked, "Because of the wording in the letters, you thought Ms. Random,"—Shapiro turned back and gestured toward me— *"this little woman* might engage in physical violence at the church? Is that right?" Sitton, now righteously defending himself, said defiantly "She might. It's not all muscle."

"Were you afraid of physical violence from Walter Alsky or Clifford Bagwell?" Still trying to imply that he had superior knowledge about such things, Sitton answered, "They were older gentlemen, but when one reached into his pocket to pull out his cell phone, I didn't know what he was going to pull out of his pocket."

"Is it your testimony that you were actually concerned that either of those gentlemen was going to pull out a weapon?" Sitton, still defiant, tipped his head back, looked down his nose, and said, "I had no idea."

There were no further questions for Howard the Hero.

Having seen me, Walter, and Clifford, it must have appeared ludicrous to everyone in that courtroom to think that one of us would carry a weapon, let alone pull it out of a pocket to harm

Martin, Howard Sitton, or anyone else, on the steps of a church.

After the jurors were released until Monday, the rest of that day was spent on motions by the defense, on jury instructions, and admissible evidence. The results of those motions would become critical to my lawsuit. The Diocese of El Camino Real had already prepared a Motion for Non-suit, meaning that if they were successful, my suit against them would be dismissed. As soon as all evidence was presented by both sides on Monday, they would ask Judge Dauphine to dismiss the Diocese. Neil told me about their motion before I left the court, but I was feeling so much better by the end of the week than I had been during the first few days, that I didn't want anything to spoil it, and I put it out of my mind. Not only that, but Judge Dauphine, after hearing what our many witnesses testified to, seemed to be giving us somewhat more appropriate rulings, and I thought there was no way she would grant their motion.

For the first time in four years, I was looking forward to attending a party—for Walter's 90th birthday. Clifford had invited more than 100 people to a celebration at the Carmel Women's Club. Everything was beautifully catered, the decorations were unique, tables were set with linens and fresh flowers, and there was a live band for dancing. Several of Walter's closest friends gave tributes to him, which were clever and entertaining. My friend Carole had remarried in 2004 and no longer lived in Carmel, but she and her husband came for the party, as well as Walter's niece and family from Los Angeles. Joan Fontaine was there, and it would not be an exaggeration to say that "everybody who was anybody" attended. City and county officials were there, including our popular county sheriff, Mike Kanalakis wearing his usual boots and black cowboy hat. The entire mood of the celebration was pure joy and camaraderie.

By a mix-up in the seating arrangement, and then a second mix-up in trying to remedy the first one, I ended up at the same table as Adrianne. When Carole realized where I was sitting, she became very concerned because Adrianne still continued to made it a point to rudely and obviously snub me. The first time had been almost four years earlier at the same Christmas party where Walter had walked away from me when he'd been introduced. That time, when I'd said hello to Adrianne, she didn't reply, didn't even look at me, got up from her chair, and walked away. I had been so shocked and hurt, that I ended up in tears while Carole tried to console me away from the other guests. By now, at Walter's party, I knew what to expect from her—and I didn't care. She stayed true to form and spoke to each of the other eight people at the table, without ever acknowledging my presence. I actually found it amusing to watch her do it because it required considerable care to keep turning her head in just the right direction to avoid me. The truth was being publicly told and, except for Adrianne, the other guests reacted to me with enthusiasm and comments of support.

The tide of my life was slowly but surely turning positive. There were still detractors of course, those like Howard Sitton who simply refused to believe the truth. At the dinner party that Jo Howard had referred to in her testimony before she was cut off, she was about to say that only two days earlier, there had been a woman guest—a parishioner from St. John's—who refused to believe anything bad about Fr. Martin, no matter what was said in the courtroom or that Jo told her. She, like Mr. Sitton, simply could not accept the truth, and she staunchly believed Martin and trusted his hand-picked vestry members, who had closed in a protective circle around him.

The woman, whom I have known for years, said it was a shame what was going on (the trial), and it was sad for Fr. Martin that I was "dragging him over the coals." Another woman that I knew from the Altar Guild, who was fully convinced that Martin had lied, still lamented to me, personally, that it was "so sad" that I sued him. Apparently, I should have kept quiet about it and done nothing to defend myself. I thought that was taking

Christian forgiveness a little too far, but didn't try to convince them otherwise because it would have been pointless. Walter's birthday party had made it clear to me that my public banishment was over, and it no longer mattered what the remaining loyalists to William Martin thought or believed.

CHAPTER SEVENTEEN

# Lest Ye Be Judged

On Saturday, there was no big headline or lengthy story in the *Herald*, but a weekend columnist known as Professor Toro reported on Ms. Fontaine's appearance at the trial with the heading, "Screen Star Fontaine Shines on the Stand." His first paragraph was, "Anticipation became anticlimactic Friday when defense attorneys blocked the testimony of screen star Joan Fontaine in the slander trial against a local Episcopal priest. But she got in some good lines anyway."

On Monday morning, day six of the trial, the attorneys all filed supplemental briefs, and Shapiro requested that Judge Dauphine take judicial notice of the Priest Discipline section of the Episcopal Church Cannons, Exhibit 61, which she had kept out during Fr. Martin's testimony. She "deferred her ruling on the matter." It seems that she not only wanted that knowledge hidden from the jury's eyes, she didn't even want to see it herself. If she actually read it, she might have been obliged to change her previous ruling and admit it as evidence against the El Camino Real Diocese.

Mr. Swartz had concerns regarding a Carmel *Pine Cone* article that referred to another lawsuit against Fr. Martin. The heading was, "Lawsuit against priest is his second for alleged defamation." The suit had been filed approximately a year earlier by Dale Howard because of outrageous and completely false statements Martin had made to me and other church members about Dale's legal practice. When interviewed by the *Pine Cone* as to whether the lawsuit would proceed, Dale said, "No further action has been taken. As to whether I will or not, I haven't made a lot of decisions about it."

We next called Fr. Christopher Creed who had conducted the Standing Committee's non-investigation. Creed is a small, mousey-looking man who, at his deposition, had leaned progressively closer to his attorney, like a child seeking parental protection. As he now sat alone in the witness chair, he appeared pathetically weak and not at all what one would expect, based on the confident and authoritative tone of the letter he had written to me—or, more accurately—the letter that an attorney had written and he signed on the pretense that he had written it. Feelings of contempt overwhelmed any sympathy I might have felt for the crumpled, little, frightened fraud in the witness chair.

After several preliminary questions, Shapiro inquired how he first learned that I had accused Martin of making disparaging and untrue statements. His answer was *almost* as fascinating as some of William Martin's had been. He said, "I have no recollection—current recollection—of that time, but knowing of the events of the spring of '05, I think that all of my knowledge about that would have come from that time. *And from seeing whatever it was that I saw, whenever I saw it.*"

Listening to some of the incoherent, rambling explanations of some of the witnesses supporting the defense, I concluded that they were no more than ordinary bullies who'd been caught. By hiding behind their pious church titles, priestly costumes, and authorities, they could bully and threaten me, but when exposed to the light of truth, they did what all cowards and bullies do. They crumbled.

In response to the obvious question, "And did you, or as far as you are aware, any member of the Standing Committee, ever make any effort to determine whether William Martin had falsely accused Rayn Random of stalking him?" Fr. Creed's answer was an amazingly unconcerned and detached, "No," without even a touch of embarrassment, much less the shame he should have felt.

"Did the Standing Committee do *anything* to investigate Ms.

Random's claims, other than have a conversation with William Martin and a telephone conversation with Ms. Norton," Creed, again, with not the slightest sign of embarrassment, replied, "That's all I'm aware of." He was the person in charge of the investigation and he couldn't even recall if the Standing committee met as a committee to discuss the fruits of the "investigation." He said that he communicated the results of the investigation to Ann Wright, President of the Standing Committee, but as for the others on the committee, he said he had no recollection. "And as far as you are aware," Shapiro asked, "did any member of the Standing Committee, other than you, take any steps whatsoever to investigate the truth or falsehood of Ms. Random's complaints about William Martin?" Again, Creed couldn't remember—a presumable—no.

After Creed, David Jones, who had refused me the Communion wine, was the next, and last, witness. He was the only witness that the defense called to the stand, except for Howard Sitton whom we called, and they also called. Their presentation of evidence in William Martin's defense consisted mainly of their cross examination of our witnesses in an attempt to discredit them and me.

Mr. Jones admitted that he had not been aware of any disruptive behavior on my part, but then added, incredibly, that if a parishioner *accurately* accused a rector of lying, that would be "disruptive behavior."

I couldn't believe what I'd heard him say. That it would be disruptive for a parishioner to tell the truth about the church priest. He also testified that it was Martin who had directed him to refuse me the wine. Martin had claimed it was David Jones' decision.

There were no more witnesses, and after jurors were released for the day, arguments were presented by Mr. Lauria regarding the Diocese of El Camino Real's motion for non-suit. Shapiro presented arguments against the motion. And then Judge

Dauphine announced her decision, "The court, Pursuant to Civil Code of Procedure section 581.c, grants the diocese motion for non-suit."

Judge Dauphine had ordered that the diocese be released from any and all liability in the lawsuit. Furthermore, she ordered *me* to pay their court costs. When Shapiro demanded the reason for releasing the diocese, she told him that we had *failed to prove that the Diocese had the authority to discipline or dismiss Fr. Martin.* The reason we failed to prove it is *because she had kept out the evidence that would have proved that the Diocese had the authority to discipline or dismiss Fr. Martin.*

It should have been left for the jury to decide whether or not the diocese was liable, based on that very evidence. I believe she intended to keep it out—as she so quickly and abruptly did when Martin was testifying—so that she would later have the grounds to grant the non-suit motion that the Diocese would routinely file after all testimony had been presented. Why else? There had been no issue of privilege, no violation of confidentiality, no ecclesiastical reason or *anything* to justify blocking it. In fact, a year later, the new bishop of the El Camino Real Diocese would issue a letter effectively proving her authority and the authority of the Diocese to discipline or dismiss priests, and she cited the sections of the Episcopal Cannons which spelled it out.[31] Why would Dauphine want to protect bishops—the church officials who have complete authority over priests—their life-long careers, and their promotions within the church? I could make a pretty good guess.

The Monterey *Herald* made it the front page headline on June 25, day seven of the trial: "Judge whittles scope of case against priest." By excusing the Diocese completely, Judge Dauphine had left only three issues for the jury to decide:

Whether William Martin had slandered me when he claimed that I tried to lure him into my hot tub.

---

31     Bishop Mary Gray Reeves letter appears on the last page.

Whether William Martin had slandered me when he claimed that I had stalked him.

Whether William Martin had committed fraud in signing the admission, knowing that he intended to deny it later.

The operative law regarding the hot tub issue was written in 1872. As it's written, the jury would have to decide whether that statement imputed "a want of chastity" to me. The dictionary definition of chastity includes reference to virginity. The jury would have to mentally modernize its meaning in today's context. If they didn't, and interpreted it literally, I would already have lost before they even entered the jury room. I'd been married for thirty-five years and given birth to a child.

The insurance which protected the defendants financially, if the jury's decision went against them, did not cover punitive damages. If the jury found that Martin was guilty of "malice," he would have to personally pay an award which would be based on his personal assets.

Judge Dauphine refused to submit to the jury the question of whether St. John's Church had acted with malice. *Once again,* she ruled that we had not presented evidence of malice or fraud as to St. John's, and therefore the church and its officers could not be held liable for punitive damages. Several legal observers have since told me that her ruling was wrong because it had been clear that the St. John's Church vestry had been fully aware of Martin's false statements about me and my claim that they were false, as evidenced in the admission William Martin had signed. Pamela Norton, a member of the vestry and Senior Warden, testified that she believed that Martin had slandered me. Howard Sitton, also a member of the vestry and a Senior Warden, said he had read Martin's admissions and yet did nothing to confirm or question them, other than ask William Martin, who gave him no answer. Anita Steel had testified that the vestry knew. They knew, just as the El Camino Diocese knew, and just like the diocese—they chose to do nothing even though they, themselves, also had the authority to discipline or even fire William Martin. Instead, they excused, protected, and covered for him to the extent of passing a resolution that he and his actions were never to be questioned—ever.

We were down to closing arguments, and Neil would have to deliver a Pulitzer Prize-winning one to overcome the now even greater odds against us. He went first, and after thanking the jury, this is part of what he told them: "I also want to acknowledge that this case is in many respects a difficult case. I told you when we were doing jury selection that it was going to be more interesting than an intersection collision. And it is. But it's also difficult because it involves a lot of emotions. I'm surprised by the number of people that have been here.

"This case is not about religion, per se. It's not about an attack on any religion or anybody's religion. One might think from the crowd that's been here that there is an entire religion under attack. But it's not. This is a case about slander and it's brought against one human being and his employer. It's just that simple.

"The law that applies is no different than if the slanderer was a store manager at Macy's and the suit was against that store manager and Macy's. A priest certainly has more power to harm a reputation and to cause pain, but the legal standards by which you should judge his conduct are exactly the same as they would be if he were the manager at Macy's.

"The key issue in this case is who is telling the truth, William Martin or a whole string of other people. The evidence on the key issue of who is telling the truth…is overwhelming. It establishes that William Martin lied. William Martin told lies about Rayn Random. William Martin lied to the parishioners. William Martin lied to the vestry of St. John's,…and he lied when he got Rayn Random to sign a mutual release."

"I think the evidence also shows very clearly that William Martin lied sitting on that witness stand. You heard him say that he never said any of those things. You heard from what I called a veritable parade of witnesses testify to the contrary."

Shapiro talked about the true progression of the situation, from my beginning friendship with Martin to when the friendship changed…"When Rayn Random sent this note[32] in mid march of 2003, everything changed. It's exhibit 45 and you'll be able to look at that in the jury room. Right after Exhibit 45 was sent, Rayn Random learned that William Martin had told Frank Reynolds at St. John's that she had tried to lure him into a hot tub, and she made inappropriate sexual advances toward him. She wrote to William Martin and said 'stop telling these lies.'

"You heard testimony from people that they considered those letters disruptive. But all she was doing was standing up for herself, and telling Reverend Martin, don't tell lies about me. Wouldn't you have done the same thing? I would.

"The evidence is clear that he was saying that she was stalking him and that he had a restraining order against her. If that had been me, I would not have reacted terribly well to that. She just wanted it stopped. She didn't want to sue anybody. She wanted him to admit that he had made these false statements, apologize for them, and that was all she asked.

"One of the issues you're going to have to decide is whether William Martin made false statements to enter into the mutual release, Exhibit 1. There is no question that he made admissions and apologies in Exhibit 1 just to avoid being sued. He knew that if he didn't make those admissions and apology, she would sue him for slander. And I think from the evidence you've heard, he had a good reason to think he probably would have lost. There's no question that he intended to recant his admission as soon as the settlement agreement was signed, and that's exactly what he did."

Shapiro did an excellent job of explaining the rest of the events that happened even after Martin had signed the admissions.

"William Martin sat on that witness stand and swore under oath that he never told anyone that Rayn Random stalked him. He swore under oath that he never told anyone that he had gotten a restraining order against Rayn Random or she harassed him with so many phone calls that he had to change his number. The witnesses tell a very, very different story."

After a further review of the evidence, Shapiro brought up the question on everyone's mind and the one that had puzzled me for four years: "Why did he start this campaign of defamation? I don't know that we'll ever know. We know from Ms. Random's testimony that he told her personal things about himself at a dinner at his house in October of 2001, but that she's never told anybody exactly what he said. She kept his confidence. She could have revealed that, but she chose not to because that would not be proper. We may never know for sure why he started making these statements. Ultimately it really doesn't matter. What matters is that he did."

Shapiro then addressed the chastity wording of the law, the statute written in 1872, and then he asked the question: "Do you think the statement 'she tried to lure me into the hot tub,' bolstered by the statement 'she made inappropriate sexual advances' leads people to believe that Ms. Random's conduct was unchaste? Do you think that the statement 'she tried to lure me into the hot tub,' in the context in which you heard it, suggests a want of chastity on the part of Rayn Random? And, if there's any doubt in your mind as to how people understood that, remember the testimony of Walter Alsky when he first met Rayn Random, he testified he asked himself, 'What is that slut doing here?' Where did he derive that do you think?

"Rayn Random testified how people turned away from her and some still do. Rayn Random was painted by William Martin as a stalker, a sexually obsessed woman, and by his lawyer as psychotic and as dangerous. I don't think there is any question that those statements harmed her reputation significantly. There is also no evidence that her reputation, other than this, was anything but sterling. And you know that the defendants looked for anything they could find. They asked her about a small claims court action she brought in Santa Clara County in 2001. They obviously searched for anything they could find. They found nothing."

In closing, Shapiro addressed the last issue of malice. "You are also going to be asked to decide whether William Martin acted with malice, fraud or oppression. And, the Court will define those for you. But, generally speaking, they mean despicable conduct in one form or another. For you to find fraud, malice or oppression, it must be clear and convincing evidence. I think the evidence supports that finding.

"It's very interesting that in this case, several witnesses talked about Exhibit 33 and about what Rayn Random said at the end of that letter that she wrote to William Martin in 2003. She wrote, 'Your actions have been deliberate, unjustifiable and designed to hurt and insult and humiliate me publicly. Your behavior as a friend is despicable. As a priest, it is unconscionable.'

"David Jones and Howard Sitton said she was behaving disruptively for saying so. All she was doing was being in their view an uppity woman who just wouldn't take the slander and slink away with her tail between her legs. The reality is, that the lies told by William Martin and his treatment of Rayn Random were, as a friend despicable, as a priest it was unconscionable.

"Please make them understand that."

Then it was the Defenses's turn to defend the indefensible. The course they chose was to try to make the jury think that none of this amounted to more than harmless every day gossip, that I didn't want to let go, and I was just a silly woman to take the whole thing so seriously. Fr. Martin was an innocent victim and had no motive other than to bring peace to a situation in which he had personally played no part.

The theme that LeVangie stressed was that William Martin was only expressing opinions, not making statements as facts, "If the statements were made, and they were made in any context, but they were Father Martin's opinion, it's not slander.

He compared the situation to a game that people play at

camp called the telephone game. "You sit a bunch of people in a row and you say one thing to somebody's ear and you keep saying it around the campfire...and you see what comes out at the other end. You see how close it is to what it started as. And usually, when people play that at camp fire, it's pretty funny. You say something simple, the cherries are red...and the next thing you know, they're saying Johnny is dead." Then he cited what he said was a famous example from British military history where the statement was, "Quick, we need reinforcements." No reinforcements came because what the person heard was, "we're going to a dance."

Then Mr. LeVangie covered his version of damages: "And although I always like it when people agree with me, I understand people don't sometimes. And it's an important thing that you'll hear in the jury instructions if for some reason you believe there is responsibility in this case by Fr. Martin, what she's entitled to is called nominal damages plus any other damages they have proven. Nominal damages are generally considered a dollar. I submit to you that there is absolutely no damage to this woman's reputation because of these two statements. None."

I was back to being "she" and the "woman," again.

On the question of punitive damages, "You have to be pretty dang sure he did it on purpose to hurt her. Intentional misstatement of fact meant to hurt the person. And I don't have much doubt about it. There's been no evidence of that. None. Zero."

He concluded with the theme he'd stressed throughout his argument, "Peace in the church. Fr. Martin tried to bring peace to this church in March of 2005 when he signed Exhibit 1, the mutual release. Rayn Random has not allowed peace to come to this church. Please bring peace to this church. Thank you."

Swartz spoke next, saying that he would "try to pull all of what's been said before me together and into some sort of a framework for you to consider...when you begin deliberating later today.

"Ms. Random has filed this lawsuit, opening a door to her personal life, opening a door to her home, opening a door to the home of William Martin, and opening a door to St. John's Chapel. We tried desperately *to go into these doors,*[33] but Ms. Random has asked us, so let's go."

Much of what he said was derogatory of me, such as, "Rayn Random. What kind of woman is she? I think she likes to be the center of attention. We ask ourselves is she really that concerned about her reputation? And if she was so concerned, would she have filed this complaint?

"Ms. Random is a paralegal who knows how to sue and who to sue. And in 2000, she moved to Monterey and joined St. John's Chapel. She buys a nice home (Mr. Swartz had never been in my home—at least to my knowledge, or by my invitation) with a Jacuzzi and meets a handsome young preacher who has also just moved to Monterey. The preacher and Ms. Random become friends. Ms. Random begins giving money to the church."

Swartz's timeline was completely misleading. I began attending St. John's seven months before William Martin arrived, didn't become acquainted with him until ten months after that, and had already been donating thousands of dollars for a year and a half. Swartz, under immunity while in the courtroom, was free to disregard facts and even to slander me, which he repeatedly did.

When Swartz talked about the hot tub, he said: "*It's rather embarrassing talking about,*" accompanied by a shy and embarrassed look. I almost burst out laughing. It was Mr. Swartz's own fabricated, lurid versions of my behavior that should have embarrassed him.

He said, "So if she's proved all of the above, the law assumes that her reputation has been harmed. Without further evidence

---

33      I believe he meant to say "We tried desperately *not* to go into these doors." Without making any accusations, I thought it an interesting slip of the tongue considering that someone tried desperately to go *into* my office door.

of damage, Rayn Random is entitled to a nominal sum such as one dollar, or such greater sum as you believe is proper for the assumed harm to her reputation under the circumstances. One dollar.

"That's what the court will read to you. You have the authority to award her one dollar if you believe she has proved each and every element of a case for slander.

"People can't sue just because they feel rejected or let down by a friend, or have their feelings hurt. People can't or should not sue because they hear gossip. Folks should be held to the agreements they make. In America, any person, even if they are a priest, has a right to be left alone when he feels uncomfortable or threatened." Then he reiterated the urging that the jury should allow St. John's to become a peaceful place again and issue a judgment in favor of St. John's. He closed with, "Thank you."

Shapiro had the final word, and he reminded the jury of a prediction he'd made that the defense lawyers would circle around the perimeter, "and would not deny that Martin told those lies," but would instead, try to trivialize them—which they did. He said that Swartz had mentioned the Cost Plus case "like that's some kind of shakedown. She broke three teeth on olives. There was a warning label on the *bottom* of a 5-pound jar. You'll have the stuff in exhibits EE through GG. She got $6,000. of which, $4250. went to pay her medical bills. That's not an issue in this case. But, they keep bringing it up.

"They tried to trivialize Reverend Martin's statements by saying he's a comedian. Do you think anybody who testified from that witness chair about what Martin said thought he was joking?

"Mr. LeVangie said it's like the game of telephone. No, it's not. This is real life.

"They said repeatedly that Ms. Random didn't want peace at St. John's, that she was the one that kept this alive. The testimony from the Steels was that William Martin kept this alive by continuing the same statements after the mutual release, as before.

"They trivialized her reputation and trivialized the damage done to her by claiming 'Well, we don't know exactly what was said.' There is no confusion about what William Martin said, and no confusion about the context in which he said it. And it is context which gives words meaning.

"They tell you no, there's no evidence of malice. I don't know. Seems to me that three years of repetitive lies shows intention to hurt, particularly when repeated even after William Martin signed the agreement to supposedly 'bring peace.' Then why has he continued to make the same lies that he made before?"

Effectively, Shapiro argued all their points about slander vs. opinion, and said that their claims smacked of blaming the victim. "I find it offensive when people blame the victim.

"Andrew Swartz said that this case is about revenge. It is not. It is about vindication of a reputation. Rayn Random's reputation was harmed by false statements. It's not about revenge. It's about her trying to vindicate her reputation.

"Make her whole again. Please."

After that, Deputy Paul Butterfield was sworn to take charge of the jury and they began their deliberations at 11:26 AM. Throughout the day they had a few questions, and after discussing them with the attorneys, Judge Dauphine went to the jury room to answer their questions. At 5:00 PM, the jurors were released for the day.

# CHAPTER EIGHTEEN

# The Wheat from the Chaff

I can't describe how I felt while we waited for the jury's decision because I hardly felt anything. I was in an emotional vacuum and my emotions floated around weightless in space. I felt drained of everything, even the ability to think, and there was nothing at that moment on which to base any feelings. There was no testimony to anticipate, and there were no angry, cold stares to confront. Everything was suddenly silent, physically, as well as emotionally and spiritually. The attorneys stayed at the court to wait, but I went home after the jury left to begin its deliberations. Neil phoned to let me know what the jury had inquired about and, again, when they were excused for the day.

Although I had no idea what an out-of-body experience was like, I imagined it must be similar to my feeling that I was a detached observer. I took care of my dogs and my cat, and the microwave cooked dinner for me. I phoned a few friends to let them know the jury was still out, and I watched television without paying any attention to what was happening. Reading was impossible because I couldn't concentrate on anything, so I wandered around my house doing nothing that mattered. When it finally got late enough, I went to bed and watched the news and Jay Leno. The only feelings I had were resignation and exhaustion.

The next morning, June 27, the *Herald* front page headline read, "Priest case goes to jury." The sub-heading was, "Statements indicate woman will win suit." I didn't subscribe to the paper, so I wasn't aware of it until later. Virginia Hennessey, the *Herald* reporter, wrote, "The verdict is not in, but a jury has apparently decided that the pastor of an Episcopal church in Monterey slandered a parishioner by telling others that she was a sexually obsessed stalker." She continued, "Late Tuesday, the jury hearing civil allegations by Rayn Random against the Rev. William Martin asked for the court's direction in the 'awarding of past non-economic damages.'

"'That means they're going to give her money,' Monterey attorney Andrew Swartz told a representative of St. John's Episcopal Church which is also being sued in the case. Just before 5:00 p.m. the jury asked Judge Dauphine if it could 'say a dollar amount plus legal fees.' Dauphine said she told the jury it could not address legal fees. The jurors quit for the day without reaching a decision."

I didn't go to the court the next morning because Neil was there and he would call me as soon as the jury reached a decision. The clerk's minute notes for that day record that "At 9:08 AM all jurors present, the jury continues to deliberate. At 9:30 AM all litigants are present in court. At 9:55 AM the court is informed that a verdict has been reached.

Clerk's notes state that, "Out of the presence of the jury and court reporter, discussions are had between the court and counsel in chambers and are not reported.

"Out of the presence of the jury, but back in the presence of the courtroom, discussions took place regarding the possibility of the trial continuing as to the single issue of punitive damages, depending on the jury's answer to section 3 of the verdict form.

"With all litigants and William Martin present in court, the jury was seated. Jury foreperson, Benton Horn, passed the verdict to the court clerk.

"The clerk read: We the jurors in the matter of Rayn Random versus William Martin, an individual, and the Rector, Wardens and Vestrymen of St. John's Chapel, a California corporation, answer the questions submitted to us as follows.

*SECTION 1*

QUESTION 1: Did William Martin make a false representation of a material fact to Rayn Random to induce her to enter into the Mutual Release, Exhibit 1?

ANSWER: YES

QUESTION 2: Did William Martin know that the representation was false, or make the representation recklessly and without regard for its truth?

ANSWER: YES

QUESTION 3: Did William Martin intend that Rayn Random rely on the representation?

ANSWER: YES

QUESTION 4: Did Rayn Random reasonably rely on the representation?

ANSWER: YES

QUESTION 5: Was Rayn Random's reliance on William Martin's representation a substantial factor in Rayn Random entering into the Mutual Release, Exhibit 1?

ANSWER: YES

*SECTION 2*

QUESTION 1: Did William Martin make any of the following specific statements about Rayn Random?

(a) Rayn Random stalked me.

(b) Rayn Random tried to lure me into her hot tub

ANSWER: YES

QUESTION 2 (a)  Did any person to whom statement (a) was made reasonably understand that the statement was charging Rayn Random with having committed the crime of stalking?

ANSWER: YES

QUESTION 2 (b)  Did any person to whom statement (b) was made reasonably understand that the statement was imputing to Rayn Random a want of chastity?

ANSWER: YES

QUESTION 3 (a)  Did any such person reasonably understand statement (a) as a statement of fact?

ANSWER: YES

QUESTION 3 (b)  Did any such person reasonably understand statement (b) as a statement of fact?

ANSWER: YES

QUESTION 4: Was either statement made substantially true?

ANSWER:  NO

QUESTION 5: Did William Martin fail to use reasonable care to determine the truth or falsity of any such statement?

ANSWER: YES

QUESTION 6: What are Rayn Random's damages?

(a) Past non-economic loss including shame, mortification, emotional distress or hurt feelings and harm to Rayn Random's reputation?

ANSWER: $148,500.00

(b) Future non-economic loss including shame, mortification, emotional

Distress or hurt feelings and harm to Rayn Random's reputation?

ANSWER: $ 0

TOTAL $148,500.00

*SECTION 3*

QUESTION 1: Was William Martin acting within the course and scope of his employment by St. John's?

ANSWER: YES

QUESTION 2: Has Rayn Random proved by clear and convincing evidence that William Martin acted with malice, oppression, or fraud in making any statement you have responded to with a "yes" in Section 2, Question 1 of this verdict form?

ANSWER: YES

Signed: Benton Horn, Presiding Juror; Dated: 6-27-07"

The jury was poled at the request of Mr. LeVangie, and each juror stated how he or she voted on each question.

The jury was then informed that the trial would continue as to the punitive damages claim against William Martin. They would have to remain to hear arguments as to what would be the dollar judgment against him for the finding of malice. The judgment would be based upon his financial condition and assets, with the decision and amount decided by the jury. They would have to listen to more testimony about Martin's financial status, and there was no way to predict how long that could last. After eight days of proceedings, the jury was tired. At 11:13 when they were released for a morning break, Neil suggested to me that rather than go through another trial and keep the jury any longer, we could propose a settlement.

I had won a battle that history indicated I would surely lose. Neil had prevailed against three attorneys, a judge—who I am completely convinced was not only incompetent, but had her own agenda—and all the church authorities and power they could muster against us. The jury had seen through all of it. I owed it to them to let them be released from anything further.

I offered to accept $1,000 as damages from William Martin, which I volunteered to donate to animal welfare on the condition that the matter ended there, no post-trial motions, no appeals, and judgment paid. It was a greater benefit and a kindness to William Martin than he deserved, but my concern was for the jurors, not him. Martin agreed, and the court was informed that a settlement had been reached. It was entered into the record as part of the final judgment, and the parties each paid their own attorney fees and costs, except that I had to pay the Diocese's court costs in addition to my own. The jury was brought back in and informed that the remaining issue of punitive damages had been settled, and that their service was complete.

When the jurors were discharged at noon, I impulsively stepped over to the jury box and, as each juror stepped down,

I held out my hand and thanked them. I didn't know if that was proper, but I didn't care. By that time, the tears wouldn't stay back any longer, although I managed to hold them in reasonable check. I will never forget how each of them looked at me. I believe they understood my gratitude to them, and even better, they clearly understood what they'd heard and witnessed in that courtroom.

After I floated home—I don't remember the drive—I didn't know what to do with myself. *It was over!* Four terrible years had ended. The truth had been told—*and believed*—at last. I felt as though I'd been allowed back into the world and I would no longer be the despicable person that William Martin had created in the minds of others.

But it was still something I couldn't quite grasp and embrace. Even though my brain kept telling me it was true, only time would allow it to seep into my psyche. Clifford arrived not long after I'd returned home, and then Walter arrived with Ms. Fontaine. We sat outside in the wonderful sunshine, relieved and joyful that justice had prevailed. The day was perfect in every way.

The next day, the *Herald* had a huge black headline that ran across the top of the front page. It said, "Priest must pay $148,500[34] for slander." During the trial the defense kept making it sound as though the slander never went beyond the church, but that was not the case. Fr. Martin cut a wide social swath of party-going all over the Monterey Peninsula, and he repeatedly spread his lies everywhere he went. Now, at last, no one—at least no one with an intelligent brain— would ever again believe him or listen to him and then say, "Poor Father Martin. I felt so sorry for him."

The sub-heading was, "$1,000 of ex-parishioner's award to be donated to animal welfare charity." I gave $760 to Animal Friends Welfare, an organization which takes pets that would

---

34      Neil and I wondered about the odd amount, but finally realized that they must have agreed on $150,000 and then deducted the $1500, that Martin paid for half of my earlier attorney fees.

otherwise be euthanized by the shelters, and I spent $240 to have an abandoned cat vaccinated and treated by a veterinarian. A friend adopted her.

On the next Sunday afternoon, I had a celebration party at my house and invited everyone who had stood by me during those four years, or had supported me throughout the trial. It was the most wonderful party I ever had. I felt like a new person and couldn't stop smiling, even when I was alone. Everyone goes through bad times in their lives and knows the feeling of incredible relief when that period ends, not realizing until then, how hard it really had been. That's how I felt, too, and I still wonder at times how I ever thought I could make the truth known after all the slammed doors, stone walls, and lies I encountered. But, I did, and I would do it all over again—even with an unknown outcome. I'd need Neil Shapiro, of course, because he fought a fierce battle that I couldn't have won without him. If Judge Dauphine were assigned to us, I'd disqualify her instantly, and I'd pray for jurors like the ones I'd had.

Neil received well deserved congratulations from his professional peers and his friends. The attorney who had turned me down and then told a judge that mine was a bad case congratulated Neil, but he couldn't restrain himself from letting it be known that he could have taken my case, which sounded like professional jealousy to me and his wanting to share Neil's spotlight. At a social gathering, Judge Dauphine also congratulated Neil for winning the case. Neil was gracious, but we both knew that he had succeeded in spite of her. When a reporter asked Neil why he'd agreed to take such a hopeless case, the reply he gave sums up the kind of person Neil is. He said, *"Because it was the right thing to do."*

In the following weeks, I also received many congratulations for fighting back, but the best and most memorable thing that anyone said to me was when a woman I knew only slightly, Gloria Ford, took me aside and quietly said, "You did it for all of us."

# Bishop Mary Gray-Reeves Letter

My dear friends,                                        May 11, 2008

Blessings to you of grace and peace in this season of Pentecost. Fr. Martin and I write to you to inform you of unfortunate news. Following last summer's trial, additional concerns were raised regarding Fr. Martin's suitability for ministry. I felt it my responsibility and duty under national **Canon IV.3.5** to address those concerns to the Diocesan Review Committee. As was their purview, per **Canon IV.3.11**, the Diocesan Review Committee sent the matter to the Church Attorney for investigation. The investigation was completed, the report of which shall remain confidential.

Within the report, however, were findings that indicated Conduct Unbecoming a Clergy Person, a chargeable offense under **Canon IV.1.1(j)**. Fr. Martin was given the opportunity to **submit to discipline for the matter of Conduct Unbecoming a Clergy Person** and in the good order and discipline of the church, as per **Canon IV.2.** He has chosen to submit to my discipline as his bishop. It is my decision to issue an Admonition and a Pastoral Direction to Fr. Martin, which delineates several stipulations and requirements, including that he not perform any ministerial tasks for a period of 60 days beginning May 12. During this time Fr. Martin and members of the congregation shall have no contact with one another. Supply clergy shall be responsible for Sunday worship and pastoral emergencies. Lay leaders have been assigned to mid-week worship services as well as other tasks. The vestry is the authority in all church matters during this time.

Please know that this charge of "Conduct Unbecoming a Clergy Person" does not include sexual or financial misconduct. It is my hope that Fr. Martin will successfully meet the requirements of our agreement in the Admonition and Pastoral Direction and that he shall be back at St. John's, Sunday July 13th. In the meantime, I ask that you refrain from all contact with Fr. Martin, turning your inquiries to the vestry. I will be at St. John's, Saturday morning, May 24th, between 10:00 and 11:00 a.m. to answer any questions you may have. The vestry and I have set up regular meeting times during the period of Admonition and Pastoral Direction, as well as beyond, in order to ensure that ministry and parish life continue to move forward in Fr. Martin's absence and upon his return.

This coming Sunday, Bishop Gethin Hughes, retired of San Diego, will be with you. I know that you will welcome him and that he will care for you. Please hold Fr. Martin, me and the parish in your prayers. With the help of Bishop Hughes and other clergy as well as your vestry, I believe St. John's will manage well during this period. It is important that all of you look to the future to help the healing; discussing actions in the past will not benefit the health of the parish. May we be blessed with deep Peace, wisdom, and an understanding of God's will.

Faithfully yours,
Mary Gray-Reeves
Bishop, Diocese of El Camino Real

# Epilogue

The question that I'm most often asked is, "Why did William Martin do that to you?" The only answer I can give is, "I don't know." For quite a while, I asked that question myself, but I never came up with an answer. Maybe there is no answer. Eventually, it really didn't matter to me, only the fact that he did it.

William Martin kept his position at St. John's for more than a year after the trial. In spite of the fact that the jury had found St. John's—meaning the vestry and other officers—liable, along with Martin, they apparently continued as they had before. There had been no financial consequence to them, and the only one for Martin was the $1,000 that he personally paid me as settlement for having intentionally harmed me. And of course, there was no consequence for El Camino Real Diocese because Judge Dauphine excused them from the case.

The second most asked question is, "Where is Martin now?" I didn't have an answer to that question either, until I happened upon an article in "VirtueOnLine" which said that a Fr. W. J. Martin had been made rector of a church in Mills River, North Carolina—All Saints Anglican Church.

William Martin's biography on the All Saint's web site has his photo, but he apparently no longer uses his previous name William J. Martin, as he is referred to as W. J. Martin. The biography states, "He was ordained at Christ Church Cathedral, Nassau, Bahamas in 2000 and served as Curate until 2001, when he accepted the position of Rector at *a church in California*. During his time in California, he taught Church Fathers and Medieval Philosophy at St. Joseph of Arimathea Seminary.[35] He was called as Rector to

---

35    One day a week.

All Saints Church in November of 2008." The almost eight years he spent as rector of St. John's is dismissed in just four words.

The third question I'm often asked is, "Have you gone back to St. John's?" I do have the answer to that question and it is, "No." Occasionally, I've thought I might go back, but I always change my mind. Some members of the congregation might welcome me, but there are still many people running the church who would not hesitate to show their displeasure and contempt for me. Who knows? They might still have the Red Book and call the police again. I have no desire to attend any church, and I don't feel the need. I know where God is, and that's all around me. I can pray whenever and wherever I choose. I would certainly attend a wedding, a baptism, or the funeral of a friend.

Judge Dauphine is no longer on the bench in the Monterey Superior Court located here. She has been transferred to Salinas and assigned to the Juvenile Dependency Department, Truancy Court.

I'm generally welcomed and greeted with smiles when I enter a room and I no longer fear being hurt or humiliated at social events. But, the people who had publicly treated me the worst before the trial behaved in ways that struck me as somewhat odd, after the trial. They acted as though *nothing had ever happened during the previous four years*, and they'd had absolutely no part in *the thing that never happened*. For example, I saw Stephanie Hulsey at our annual Monterey birthday celebration—Clifford had insisted that I go as his guest—and it was my first re-appearance at a public event. It was very crowded and Stephanie waved to get my attention, sent me a big smile, and mouthed the word, "Congratulations." I don't know what else I should have expected, but it struck me as odd because the last time I had seen her, both she and her husband Kevin—who was shouting threats in my face—had been standing on the St. John's steps trying to keep me out and now, *I* was expected to respond as though *nothing had ever happened*. I gave her a less than sincere smile in return, but time has changed it to a more genuine one when I see her now.

At a luncheon gathering—at Adrianne's house—I was seated next to a woman who had been one of the most blatant and haughty in snubbing me and speaking past me. She turned on the charm and kept trying to engage me in conversation. Looking at her friendly face directly in front of me, I wondered to myself if she thought that I could be so stupid as to not have noticed how she had treated me, or that I would be grateful to have regained her favor. I replied politely, but didn't feel obliged to help her assuage her conscience—that is, if she had one.

Because we have many mutual friends, I see Adrianne frequently. Neither of us has ever mentioned the past.

There is one very sad note to add. Dearest Walter died in March of 2010. His funeral Mass was celebrated at the Carmel Mission Basilica and there was standing room only.

Stephanie Hulsey sang beautifully.

# A Commentary by Neil Shapiro

One of the strangest cases in my forty years of civil litigation began with an interesting telephone call in December of 2005. The caller, a woman named Rayn Random, then 71, told me that she had been slandered repeatedly by an Episcopal priest, that she had hired a lawyer to represent her, that the parties had executed a settlement agreement in which he admitted the slander, but that he had resumed making the same statements. She wanted me to represent her and sue him.

It didn't make sense. I quizzed her for perhaps forty-five minutes trying to find the hole in her case. I knew what questions to ask; I had represented publishers and broadcasters in defending libel and slander cases for three decades and knew just about every way to defeat them. But she had a good answer for every question I asked. Her story just couldn't be right, I thought, but if by some stretch it was she might have a decent case. So I agreed to meet her. I had no intention of taking her case, but thought that I might be able to give her some sound advice and maybe point her in the right direction.

When we met at my office, she showed me the settlement agreement. Sure enough, the priest admitted the slander. I asked who could corroborate her claim that he was again telling people those same lies. She gave me names. We spoke at length about what her life would be like if she filed the contemplated lawsuit. I explained how stressful it would be for her to be involved in such a contentious process. She said that living with the slander was more stressful than a lawsuit could possibly be. I described the myriad defenses available against claims based on speech, the real risk of loss even if the statements had been made, and how she would feel if she lost. She responded that she would rather fight and lose than do nothing. I agreed to check with the people whose names she had given me, and she thanked me and left.

The calls I made confirmed some of her story, but I knew that winning her case would be difficult – and hard on her – and I decided not to take it. My heart wanted to. I felt so sorry for her and believed that there was no other decent lawyer in this community who would represent her. By any measure, she deserved to have someone stand up with her. But I knew what an uphill battle suing a priest and his church would present and that it would drain both of us. "Life's too short," I told myself. I called her. We chatted for a bit about my interviews of prospective witnesses and she asked, "will you represent me? " I opened my mouth, ready to say "no," but my heart answered instead.

The journey from that moment through the trial in June of 2007 was unlike any in my career. Three defense attorneys, one each for the priest, the church and the diocese, kept the pressure on us with a wealth of pre-trial procedures. The testimony of some members of the church vestry – essentially its board of directors – was in ways shocking, ranging from blind obedience to a misguided priest to sudden and complete amnesia to outright fabrication. Building the case and getting to trial was exhausting. The trial itself lasted eight days, but it frankly took me a month to recover. Why? The night before I put Rayn on the stand to tell her story, I slept for all of two hours. The night before closing argument I slept even less. Add in unpredictable and inconsistent rulings by the judge and three opposing counsel all taking shots at everything we did, and one pretty much gets the picture.

If I had it to do all over again, I'd do the same thing. At least outwardly, Rayn was a pillar of strength through the entire process; she kept her twin senses of purpose and humor through the long ordeal, and I admire her for that. She had been pushed around for too long, and just wasn't going to be pushed anymore without fighting back. In the end she received the vindication so long in coming. Helping her achieve that vindication was a gift to me. We embarked together on a difficult road, Rayn playing her role and me playing mine. We remained resolute, and in the end were rewarded. I have been a litigation lawyer for a long time, and I have to say that it just doesn't get much better than that.

## ABOUT THE AUTHOR

While still in high school, Rayn was awarded scholarships to the Minneapolis Art Institute and then continued her art studies at the University of Minnesota and the University of the Americas in Mexico City. After an award winning career as a marketing director, she retired to become a stay at home mom. Eventually she returned to college to study law, finished with honors, and opened a highly respected and well known paralegal firm.

Following the death of her husband, Rayn returned to the Episcopal Church and became far more involved than she had ever been before, or ever intended to be. It is that shocking, incredible, life shattering experience that she relates in her non-fiction book, *Cocktail Party Priest,* which will soon be followed by two novels already waiting in the wings: *Evil at the Altar* and *Silent Partners.*

Rayn has served as a volunteer Court Appointed Special Advocate for abused, neglected and abandoned children and been active in several organizations. She lives with her German Shepherd, Darius, and her rescued Calico cat, Amber.

CHECK OUT MY WEB SITE:
PHOTOS, BLOG, COMMENT
www.therandomcompany.net

# UPCOMING NOVELS BY RAYN RANDOM

***Evil at the Altar***  Newly ordained an Episcopal priest, Edward McAllen appears to have it all...a Yale education, parents with standing and respect in St. Paul society, and his grandmother's fantastic fortune to inherit. With the help of his bishop—and his father's generous donations to the church—Edward embarks on a bright future with his chaste and pretty bride at his side. But Edward has a secret life; one that threatens to destroy him if exposed. So, when a homeless man accidentally discovers the truth, Edward is thrown into a frightening spiral in which he will stop at nothing, including betrayal, theft, blackmail, and even reckless murder to save himself. His best friend pleads with him stop before it's too late, but Edward will not listen and continues his headlong course to final destruction, not only of himself, but of those who are closest to him.

***Silent Partners***  California's most famous treasure that brought speculators and fortune seekers was the near 24 kt. gold discovered in the tailrace of a new lumber mill that Gen. John A. Sutter was building in 1848. Thus began the famous California Gold Rush. But, that's not the prize that has been coveted and fiercely fought over for the last 100 years. It's land and water that men have risked fortunes and reputations for. And the less that remains of them, the fiercer the battles have become. Money, power, and political connections are the weapons, and there are no rules.

Luka Sokolov, rumored to be a former member of the Russian "mafia," is one such warrior and he has a special weapon and ally: his beautiful, intelligent, and cunning daughter, Irina. To Daddy, it's a deadly serious challenge and ego trip; to daughter, it's a game. No one is off limits to be used as a pawn in their battle strategies, not even Irina's idealistic husband who has just been elected to the state legislature with the financial support of his father-in-law and the encouragement of his loving wife.

Made in the USA
Charleston, SC
16 February 2012